Vin de la' Suisse. Elle ... partagée en deu...
de superieur non ... ns le ..., ... mesme dans ...
maison de Fribourg ... par mesme moyen dans cell...
un surcrivit de bonh...

La Description

L'étenduë en   de la Principauté   la France.
auquel elle   peuplées, le la
de la Suisse   de Neufchâtel &   meilleur Vin
superieur non   point de
de Fribourg   de Valangin   dans la maiso...
urcivit de bonh   avec un

le Duc de Longueville

Son aimable frère,

le Ciel me donna

Altesse, avec tous ses — le Duc de Long...
vantages, J'ai crû —
...ont moins qu'avec — Son aimable...
...m'acorder en...

La

Description

de la Principauté la France.
de Neufchâtel & peuplées, le
de Valangin meilleur Vi
point de
dans la mais
avec un j

L'étenduë en
auquel elle
de la Suisse
superieur non
de Fribourg
urewist de honk

le Duc de Longueville

Son aimable frère,

le Ciel me donna

Altesse, avec tous ses — le Duc de Lon
vantages, J'ai crû — Son aimable
é'ont moins qu'avec — m'acorder ens
...t Essay ... lui

Unmistakably FRENCH

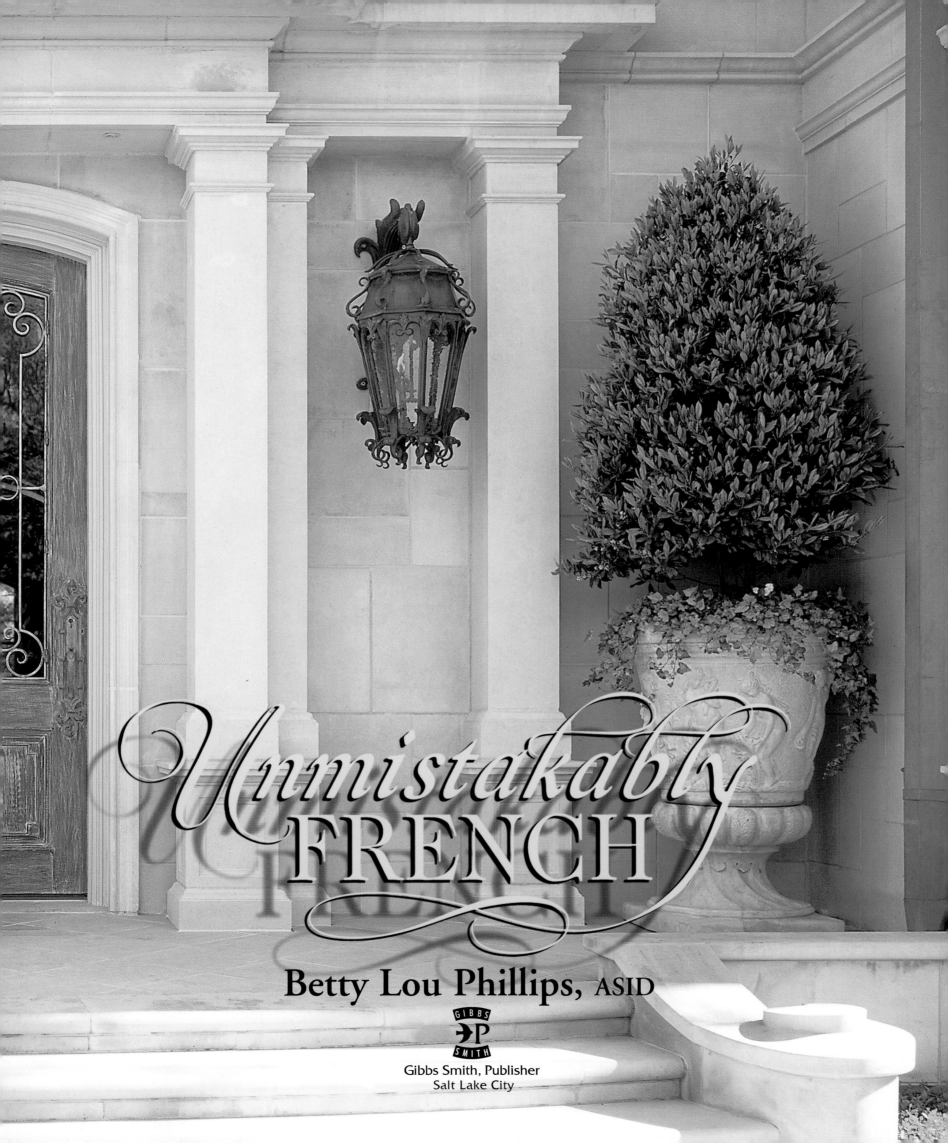

Unmistakably
FRENCH

Betty Lou Phillips, ASID

Gibbs Smith, Publisher
Salt Lake City

07 06 05 04   10 9 8 7 6 5 4 3

Published by
Gibbs Smith, Publisher
P.O. Box 667
Layton, Utah 84041

www.gibbs-smith.com
Orders: 800.748.5439

Designed by Cherie Hanson
Printed and bound in Hong Kong

Library of Congress Cataloging-in-Publication Data
Phillips, Betty Lou.
Unmistakably French / Betty Lou Phillips.—1st ed.
p. cm.
ISBN 1-58685-289-2
1. Interior decoration—United States—History—20th century. 2. Decoration and ornament—France— Influence.
I. Title.
NK2004 .P555 2003
747'.0973—dc21
2003010160

Front Jacket: Architect Robbie Fusch and designer Deborah Walker together created an ambience that appears centuries old. Fifteenth-century French Renaissance style – the reign of Charles VIII (1483–98) – inspired the Dallas, Texas, estate whose dramatic stone staircase leads to an *enfilade* of rooms.

Title Page: Insuring that all-important first impression is both positive and lasting, fixtures from Orion Antique Importers, Dallas, light the French exterior.

Opposite: With regal presence and overpowering beauty, wrought-iron gates hint at the graciousness within a private world reflecting the glory of France.

Table of Contents: A retrofitted commode takes center stage in a guest powder room with fittings from Sherle Wagner. Walls are Venetian plaster – a labor-intensive, old-world technique that requires applying a polished wax finish to achieve the look of an old Renaissance painting.

End Sheets: "French Script" by British designer Carolyn Quartermaine is available through Christopher Hyland in the D & D Building, New York City, and showrooms nationwide.

Back Jacket: A glamorous mix of drama and style awakens the senses while adding to a dressing room's allure. Antique mirrors fit snugly in doors. But the cabinets, closets, and drawers also borrow elements from eras past. Hovering over the dressing table is a carved cornice that is generations old. Eighteenth-century crowns are worthy of the setting.

Table
OF CONTENTS

Acknowledgments

Whether their home is newly constructed, creatively renovated, or lovingly restored, there is little time for any homeowner to settle in when an author trying to meet a deadline and cameras with wide-angle lenses hover behind painters with ladders and drop cloths. Yet when doors swung open to the rooms featured here, instead of an embarrassment of boxes, all was in place, though most homes had been lived in only a few weeks. Amazingly, some owners were even planning parties.

So, thank you to those who graciously welcomed us inside their corner of the world where we could oooh and applaud each look: Abby Ahrens, Doris Bass, Teresa and John Beltramo, Georgia and Michael Bennicas, Rosanna and Myron Blalock, Carolyn and David Crosswell, Stacey and Reed Dillon, Ann and Leslie Doggett, Schelley and Dana Dutcher, Linda and William Gibbons, Shirley and Alan Goldfield, Dana and William Moore, Norma and Marvin Myers, Anthony Stavish, Shelley and David Stevens, Catherine and Jeffrey Wood, Nancy and Philip Young, and more.

I am also grateful to those designers responsible for priming rooms for the spotlight while perpetuating the taste for eighteenth- and nineteenth-century French style with twenty-first-century American flair: Cathryn Chapman, David Corley, Cheryl Driver, Pamela Kay Flowers, Robert Preston Henry, John Kidd, Pryor Lancaster, Liz Lank, Dana Moore, Molly Ogden, Roberta Peters, Christina Phillips, Marilyn Phillips, Elizabeth Smith, Anthony Stavish, Shelley Stevens, Julie Stryker, Mersina Stubbs, Robert Wakefield, and Deborah Walker.

Thank you, too, to friends and family who shared their time, energy, and ideas in a search for the best of the French: Biff Agee, Teresa Beltrammo, Judy Blackman, Gillian Bradshaw-Smith, Donna Burley, Constantino Castellano, Bruno de la Croix-Vaubois, Joan Eleazor, Layne Eleazor, Rela Gleason, Sherry Hayslip, Joe Lugo, Christie McRae, Kelly Phillips, Marilyn Phillips, Mary Beth Riddle, Sandra Rouse, Tommy Rouse, Joe Salvino, Dominique Sanchot, Jayne Taylor, and Pat Wood. Also, thank you Janice Pedersen Stuerzl, the most efficient assistant, and Cherie Hanson, book designer extraordinaire.

Unmistakably French is also the result of the efforts of editor Madge Baird, whose talents helped shape this book—as well as my first children's book, *Emily Goes Wild!* May you enjoy both!

When it comes to design, style stretches to unexpected elements, including a clever invitation that fits fast-paced lives.

Opposite: A seventeenth-century Italian table sets a hospitable tone in a tasting room. Tall urns are Italian *majolica,* circa 1890. Smaller jugs and baskets are French antiques.

Introduction

In *châteaux* with the refined air for which the French are famous, there are two-story entrance halls with stone floors and sweeping staircases, *bibliothèques* fashioned from trees felled before our country was born, proper dining rooms with smoke-stained limestone fireplaces, and large, airy salons that host well-mannered ladies and gentlemen. Many *boudoirs* drift onto flower-rimmed terraces overlooking cobblestone court-yards fringed with chestnut trees, while deep, freestanding tubs bask in marble-clad bathrooms washed by the morning sun. More tellingly, though, behind most every imposing door lies a certain *je ne sais quoi* that eludes easy definition.

So what, exactly, *is* it that is set in the classical splendor of France? It's artistry, it's attitude, it's style and far more. It is a virtuous mix of panache and simplicity, taste and resourcefulness that is at once inviting, surprising, and inspiring.

Yes, we are struck by the *flair* of the French—and why not? With their self-assured approach to design and mesmerizing way of projecting a rich cultural heritage with matchless sophistication and lack of showiness, they quite rightly have captured our respect. But, then, we are not the first Americans to be so enraptured. Thomas Jefferson helped frame the French as paragons of good taste when he had

eighty-six crates of Parisian treasures—including several pieces of Sèvres porcelain once owned by Louis XVI—shipped to Monticello, his mountaintop estate in Charlottesville, Virginia, following a five-year term as minister to France (1784–89).

Five years later, Boston financier James Swan, a former American Revolutionary War colonel dispatched by the United States government, further drew attention to French sophistication and style after French Revolutionary authorities seized the contents of Versailles and other royal residences. In exchange for tobacco and firearms, he acquired a *lit d'alcove* (a splendid bed), a *bergère* (fully upholstered armchair with enclosed sides and exposed wood frame), two *fauteuils* (upholstered armchairs with open sides) and other period pieces stamped by the celebrated Jean-Baptiste-Claude Sené, who crafted furniture for Marie Antoinette's bedroom at Fontainebleau, south of Paris. The Swan collection now rests in Boston's Museum of Fine Arts.

Since the eighteenth century, much has changed in the world, of course. Yet Fine French Furnishings—or FFF, as known these days—still find Americans among their most ardent admirers. That we are intent on finding reflections fitting connoisseurs of *bon goût* is readily apparent, in fact.

Scouring renowned antique-world stops—including Paris's legendary flea markets, Hôtel Drouot auction rooms in the Ninth Arrondissement, and Left Bank shops—we marvel at the abundance of offerings while unabashedly adding to our inventories near-perfect commodes, iron beds, and slipper chairs—all more than a little alluring.

But the old-world élan of our rooms may well owe even more to secrets we have gleaned from the French. How else to explain—given our preference for juxtaposing different periods and far-flung influences in edgy ways—turning out settings *unmistakably French* worthy of France at her best?

Betty Lou Phillips, ASID
Author and Stylist

Preceding Overleaf: Rather than the expected arrangement of sofas facing each other on either side of a fireplace, they now sit back to back, balancing the lengthy room. A table found in Paris made for the 1900 Expo World Fair by the Barcelona School of Arts separates the groupings. The Aubusson is from the Stark Carpet Company, drapery hardware from Cole Smith, Dallas. Chandelier is custom. Italianate fireplace is late-eighteenth century.

Opposite: A detail of drapery hardware that permits easy access to well-tended grounds.

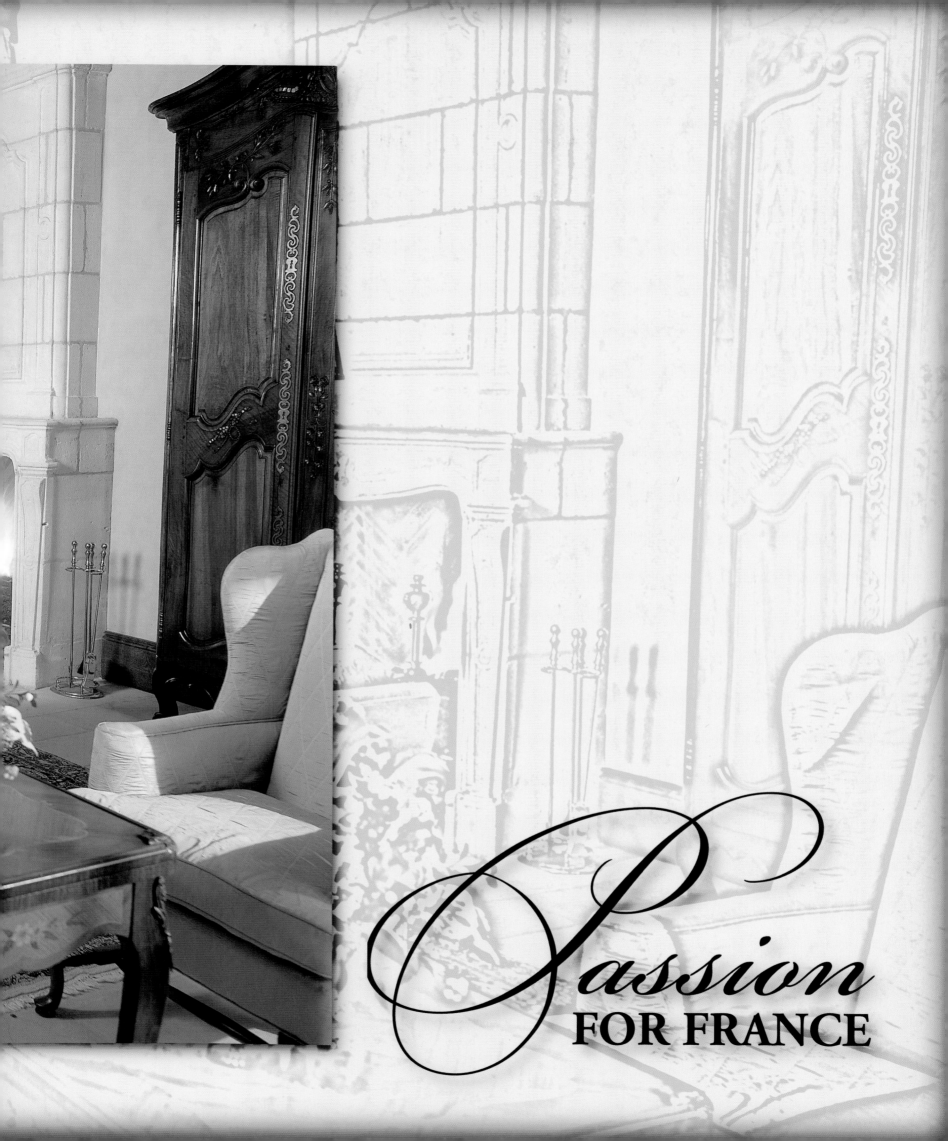

Passion
FOR FRANCE

Other nations may well envy the steadfast loyalty with which the French speak of their country, to say nothing of the admirable manner in which they guard a cultural heritage enriched by a plethora of artistic talent. For they make no secret of their love for family, affection for pets, and fervor for France, let alone suppress fierce commitment to preserving fragments of centuries past. Finding boundless inspiration in their vibrant history, it is not surprising, then, that they contend you are what you know.

Passion FOR FRANCE

The truth is, in an exam-orientated country where even three-year-olds *must* attend *école maternelle* (nursery school) in readiness for competitive grades, education lies somewhere near the very heart of identity. Approximately seventy-five daily newspapers—authoritative *Le Monde, Le Figero,* and *Libération* among them—never fail to remind readers that it is important to have a deep knowledge of France, far-reaching views of the world, and substantive opinions about the montage of issues dominating the press.

A cultural legacy that piece by piece is disappearing is widely reported by the media and therefore a topic on everybody's mind, though the government can now preempt the sale of art at auctions by exercising its right to buy historically important works at the price they have sold to a bidder.

But with a wave of tourists, architects, and decorators—speaking English and Japanese, Spanish and Italian—clamoring for French heirlooms, concern leads many *habitués* to canvas narrow cobbled streets in hope that they can prevent their national symbols from being shipped to the United States or elsewhere in the world while still within reach.

Preceding Overleaf: Speaking impeccable French is a magnificent *cheminee a trumeau,* flanked by a Louis XV towering walnut armoire and Louis XV commode, all dating back to the eighteenth century. To this day, the eighteenth century is thought the most elegant era in European history. The wood pieces are from Country French Interiors, Dallas. Wing chairs wear Coraggio.

Opposite: Reflecting grand French style is a dining room with the stateliness of an elegant *chateau.* In the glow of an eighteenth-century Regence mirror is an overdoor rescued from ruin at Saint Cloud, Napoleon and Empress Josephine's residence outside Paris. The nineteenth-century chandelier is Baccarat, the *cristallerie* founded in 1764 by writ of Louis XV.

Dashing from antiques shops on the rue Jacob, the rue des Saints Pères, and the rue de Seine to bustling sales in the Hôtel Drouot, where more than three thousand auctions are clustered annually, the French routinely bargain over rock-crystal chandeliers bearing dust, chairs wearing weathered leather, and blurry mirrors that look as if they stepped out of the eighteenth-century works of art lining noble walls; albeit, back then mirrors often cost more than the finest paintings, which is why Louis XIV's Hall of Mirrors was considered astonishing.

By all appearances, it seems unlikely that France will run out of stone garden statuary or other testaments to its storied history anytime soon. But even with all the splendid antiques gathered about, most quarters are neither intimidating nor fussy. Indeed, French people equate elegance with restraint. For them, comfort and tastefulness are paramount, not belongings that cost a queen's ransom or unwelcome attention to extravagant ways. The cardinal rule of their upbringing is: Wealth and discretion go hand in hand, which means care is taken not to trample tradition by flaunting vain indulgences that are showy

Above: An eighteenth-century wall panel – from a *chateau* outside Paris salvaged in a fire – now embellishes this ceiling.

Opposite: Helping create a memorable setting is an oil on canvas by Joseph Marie Dumas Des Combes (1813-85) from the French Barbizon School. The last in a series of four, it was shown in 1872 at the Salon des Independants in Paris, and still wears its original gilded frame bearing the exhibition tag number. Cast-iron urns are mid-nineteenth-century copies of ones found at the Chateau de Versailles. The console is from later in the century. The *putti* are dated 1776.

trappings of success, much less break the age-old cultural taboo of appearing as though living stylishly is a preoccupation in itself.

Despite the grandeur in which Louis XIV, the Sun King (1643–1715), resided in the magnificent Palace of Versailles, *grandes maisons* with seldom-used rooms, flawless jewels, or for that matter, fancy cars that reflect privilege, simply do not appeal to the sensibilities of French aristocrats. Or even to the young upwardly mobile who choose to make do with smaller accommodations, irrespective of high birth. But then, ostentatious behavior is rare at all strata of society.

Never mind the valued Aubusson and Savonnerie carpets that swathe oak *parquet de Versailles* floors laid in diagonal composite squares, or the prized tapestries ascending stately stone staircases, or even the centuries-old furniture that exercise influence on American minds in the way that French rooms often do. Quiet elegance—which cannot be bought—is the celebrated source of Gallic pride.

Making for a grand entrance are eighteenth-century oak doors that once graced an *hôtel particulier* – a private mansion with wisteria spilling over courtyard walls in the Bordeaux region of France. Lanterns are copies of nineteenth-century gas lights, made as they were more than two hundred years ago, by using the lost wax method of bronze casting called *cire perdu*, a five-thousand-year-old procedure.

THE *Art* OF LIVING

Whether looking to furnish a *château* in the Loire Valley, a getaway *folie à deux* in Bordeaux, a manor house in Normandy, or a *hôtel particulier* in Paris's historic Sixth Arrondissement, the French seldom stray from well-practiced beliefs to a wish list of riches with splashes of gilding. Inarguably, eighteenth-century furniture, sumptuous textiles, distinctive porcelains, and oil paintings in original carved-wood frames are both coveted and collected. But none is more important than the values that the people, as if by agreement, hold dear.

Granted, in a country as mosaic as France, it is not as if any list can claim to be comprehensive. There is, after all, no single way to live. And while imitation has long been the sincerest form of flattery, aesthetic visions vary widely when it comes to expressing one's inner self. Still, it seems, the French always start with some basics from which we can learn:

Quality Matters Most

Insistence on quality, many say, is in their genes—a gift inherited—which may very well be true, although it might, in fact, be acquired in childhood when most learn to recognize and value beautiful things. Either way, it hardly matters. Like father, like son; like mother, like daughter. The trait runs deep—not least because anxious parents consider it a routine part of a proper education to shepherd their children to museums, where those old enough to skip naps have more than their share of instruction in learning to distinguish between fine and mediocre; then comes understanding the difference between perfection and anything less, or, simply put, developing a taste for the finer things in life.

Preceding Overleaf: Juxtaposing architectural grandeur with French sophistication creates an extraordinarily welcoming environment. Cameron Textiles wraps the sofas in luxurious chenille while the antique Oushak rug adds warmth.

Opposite: In the dining hall of a monastery – called a refectory – meals were meant to nourish both body and soul, so monks sat on only one side of long, narrow tables arranged much like the letter "U," facing the abbot. This nineteenth-century refectory table is from the South of France. The hand-tooled leather antique chairs traveled from Brittany to Kansas City's European Express, before winding their way into this breakfast room. The chandelier once belonged to Caesar Romero.

Branching out, otherwise replacing the breakfast room's baseboards is a collection of seventy terra-cotta tiles – each ten inches wide and twelve inches tall – signed "La Tuilerie du Theil" and dated 1873. *Tuile* is the French word for tile, and a *tuilerie* is where tiles are made, thus Tuileries Garden is located on the site of an old *tuilerie*. This assortment of tiles came from Barbara Israel Garden Antiques in Katonah, New York.

Distinctive cabinetry of the butler's pantry.

Opposite: With their aristocratic good looks, Louis XIV chairs robed in Silk Road fabric surround an eighteenth-century walnut table from Italy. The Oushak rug – an Oriental of Turkish decent, dated 1890 – inspires the earth-tone palette. Plant stands are from Peter Jennings Antiques, Inc., on Melrose Avenue in West Hollywood. Fortuny-like silk frames windows.

A detail of the exquisite dining room walls that took weeks to complete. The Chinese developed the technique of stenciling around 300 B.C. Glazing adds life.

Opposite: With purple being the imperial color when Louis XVI was king, Chuck Matney Floral Design in Kansas City, Missouri, adds to the room's ambience with flowers arranged in the homeowners' vintage French containers made of lead.

During the eighteenth century, France astonished the world with her masterful artisanship, setting the standards of excellence that twenty-first-century tastemakers openly admire and by which they judge Fine French Furnishings and most everything else. Along the posh rue du Faubourg Saint-Honoré in Paris, lined with luxury boutiques and high-end antiques, and in *brocante* (secondhand) shops on quiet streets throughout the provinces, it is both well known and accepted that the French *still* are famously hard to please, three centuries later. Indeed, they expect a level of workmanship that, more often than not, only money can buy. As it is, most do not even consider stripping doors and moldings of multiple coats of paint themselves, or tackling stylish painted finishes—glazing, marbleizing, *faux bois* (wood graining), stenciling, gilding, and *trompe l'oeil* (a treatment more than a bit deceptive)—let alone performing tasks such as fixing sagging floors, repairing plastered walls, or replacing bathroom tile, which require talents they do not possess. The way they see it, professional-looking results means turning these projects over to experts with nothing less than well-honed skills.

Faced with the daunting task of returning an aging manor to splendor it has not seen for years, the conventional wisdom is that some things are better left undone rather than done poorly or given a quick fix—which is why many imposing exteriors built centuries ago are still in serious disrepair, leaving faded grandeur worthy of their stature and, yes, some proud *maisons* with mansard roofs leaking, window frames rotting, wet walls crumbling, and heating unreliable, languishing unoccupied after passing from one generation to the next.

A French inheritance law requiring that land be handed down equally to each offspring once, seemingly, satisfied everyone; now it is encountering criticism. Its approval did not consider that siblings who must share the family domain may or may not be able to entertain dreams of maintaining the estate or of paying the property taxes, much less afford to buy each other out.

Quite clearly, interiors take shape according to one's resources and definition of style, mirroring needs and habits as opposed to the times. Unlike Americans of elevated means, who often spend years installing newly acquired historical elements such as antique fireplaces and old staircases designed to turn domiciles into citified castles, the French rarely undertake earth-moving renovations or home improvements that diminish a dwelling's original cachet—never mind raze a house to make way for a mansion better suited to an affluent neighborhood.

With bold resistance to change, to say nothing of pretense, most have little interest in converting areas dripping with age into media rooms that rival the metroplex, state-of-the-art exercise rooms that require personal trainers, fancy country kitchens fitting chatty chefs, or sumptuous master bedrooms with high-tech comfort zones that pay homage to dawn-of-the-millennium American tastes. Instead, "*Le plus ça change, le plus c'est la même chose,*" or "The more things change, the more they remain the same," is an adage that most live by.

And so, offering no apologies for their relentless search for quality or appetite for elegance, furnishings are the best one can manage, testifying to one's impeccable taste while presenting one's family history. Like most people we know, the French splurge on things that are important to them and economize on others. Invariably, some find it hard to resist vintage bargains in the Marché aux Puces de Saint-Ouen, the vast weekend flea market on the outskirts of Paris, or in L'Isle-sur-la-Sorgue,

Opposite: The stone sink is old. Houston designer John Kidd and artist Rusty Arena collaborated to create the powder room walls. Around the periphery of an antique mirror thought to be from France, each monk wears a different expression. Not knowing the mirror's precise history, some like to think it dates back to Dom Perignon, the French monk who first discovered the secret to making fabled Champagne. Upon tasting the drink for the first time, he reportedly called out to his fellow monks, "Come quickly, I am drinking stars!" From the looks of it, so did they!

the once-radiant silk-weaving town cradled between branches of the Sorgue River. More, though, shun temptation and instead buy the finest furniture and household linens they can afford, willingly paying for quality over quantity, regardless of their means.

With luxury hidden in hand-tied springs of tailored, down-filled sofas, and glaring beauty in intricately carved marriage armoires, as well as deftly placed *passementerie*—the seventeenth-century term for tassels, braids, tiebacks, and other trimmings—the French are quick to point out that there are valid reasons some furnishings are more expensive than others are. Further, they say, it is pointless to complain, since you pretty much get what you pay for, considering that under French law, shops are permitted to hold sales only twice a year, in January and August.

Without fail, exquisite silks, jacquards, damasks, and velvets woven in Lyon's fabled fabric mills—and widely distributed throughout Europe and the United States—win considerable applause. Setting them apart is the way in which they cascade from towering windows and descend from *lits à la française* (canopied beds) when cut and constructed with a meticulousness approaching *haute couture*. Not that the French are apt to purchase expensive textiles and then save by fabricating curtains or bed hangings themselves, anymore than they are likely to upholster walls or undertake other tasks best executed by experts.

The past must be ever present, as writer Françoise Sagan famously noted. Filling empty rooms with shiny new furniture is all right for some people, but not for the French. To their way of thinking, it is inexcusable to live in a house full of meaningless pieces with no ties to the past or any sentiment attached, and even worse, one furnished at a hurried pace with pricey objects lacking character. Charm lies in time-honored *vaisseliers* (hutches), armoires made in scattered provincial towns, and *chiffonières* (chests of drawers) wearing original paint, collected over generations. Also central to life are carpets that are threadbare in places, tracing the history of France.

With nostalgia for bygone eras, it does not much matter, apparently, that a faithful reproduction—with detailing true to the period—often costs less than an antique holding court one hundred or more years later. There is a longstanding assumption that early pieces are superior to copies more recently crafted.

A grill unearthed by a metal detector on a Galveston, Texas, beach is now inset in a hall wall where it adds interest.

Moreover, the mind-set seems to be that it is impossible to replicate the patina of age, a distinctive luster resulting from centuries of exposure to heat, humidity, and light. In reality, there is more than a little truth to this, which may explain why the old generally wins out over the new—much to the chagrin of today's furniture makers, who long to move everyone forward in time by recognizing artistry they believe is equal to that of their predecessors. This is not to say they have given up hope. After all, they point out, for ages, French '40s furniture held no allure, mostly because it harbored memories of war and the German occupation of France, from 1940 to 1944. Yet today, it is the popular new collectible, gracing *très chic* homes featured in glossy shelter magazines.

Interiors Merit Furnishings with Presence

For centuries now, a propensity for heroic-sized pieces has held sway. Regardless that large houses throughout France have gradually given way to less spacious ones with smaller rooms, the need for imposing furnishings that lend distinction remains etched in minds, largely unchanged. And since this is the scale the eye is accustomed to seeing, it is maneuvered into enlarging its perception of an area, until somehow even cramped quarters appear larger while grand rooms become more palatial still.

Opposite: In an about-face, a laundry room proudly airs its dirty linens, making light of wash-day drudgery. But then, soaking, cleansing, rinsing, drying, and ironing clothes have come up from dismal basements – in a positive spin.

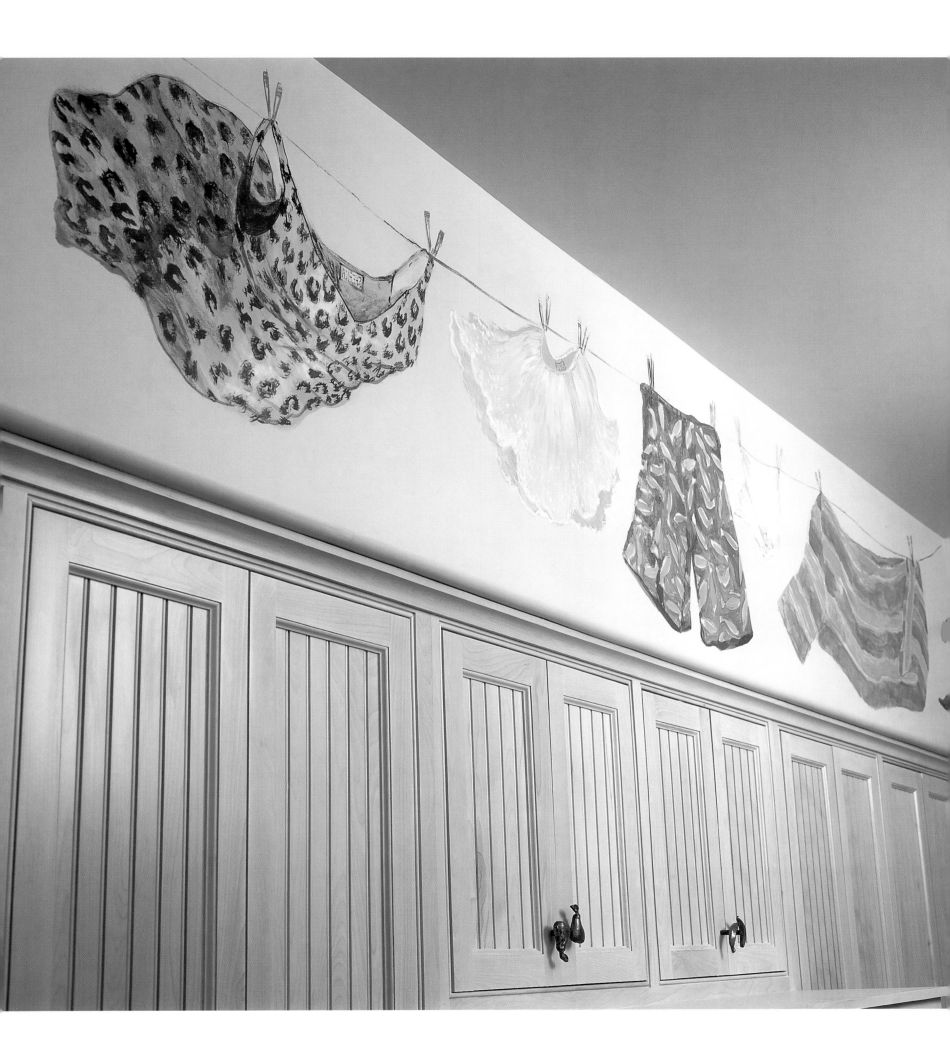

GiGi, an adored pug, parks in her favorite spot while family members consider various fabrics to recover the chair. As a homesick newlywed, Marie-Antoinette wrote her mother, Maria-Theresa of Austria, asking that she send to France the family's pugs. But even before then, the breed had become the ultimate status symbol at court.

Opposite: It can be difficult to see the beauty in an old door, but not when one comes from a stable in France.

En grand or *petit, salons* boast majestic armoires with regally curved bonnets, commodes with intriguing hardware, and splendid desks and console tables whose gracefully carved cabriole legs back up to roomy sofas. Desks and consoles are at least sixty inches long, and, more commonly, impressively longer. By French standards, when a desk or sofa table sits behind an eighty-four- to ninety-six-inch sofa, only ten inches of sofa should be exposed on a side.

Accordingly, sofas with opulent rolled arms are pleasantly plump, whereas imperial-looking *récamiers* as wide as daybeds and Louis XVI painted *canapés* (settees) that once brought splendor to *appartements* on Paris's avenue Foch are unexpectedly comforting, thanks to a mix of

Lyrical motifs resound on an island reflecting the owner's interest in music. In France, a display, or *trophee*, if one will, of painted, carved, or inlaid symbols often has historic, political, or literary overtones, usually accompanied by florals and ribbons.

Opposite: A whirlwind makeover transformed this timeworn San Francisco kitchen into a bright, sumptuous space, with color-washed walls and hand-hewn timbers that hide the room's dismal past. The center island offers extra workspace for serious cooks who revel in serving classic French cuisine.

showy pillows, stitched mainly from vintage fabrics. For the most part, the deeper the piece, the larger the throw angled invitingly in a corner reducing the depth.

Stately buffets of grand proportions (a two-piece buffet is called a *buffet à deux corps,* and one that has a series of doors is known as an *enfilade**), valued as much for their functionality as their old-world elegance, satisfy the need for storage and serving space in areas intended for entertaining.

Despite the populace tending to be rather short, men and women think nothing of serving from buffets forty to forty-two inches tall. In many minds, ease is not a priority. As befits a society awash in style, aesthetically pleasing is. And the accepted belief is that taller wood pieces are, indeed, more chic.

Family Heirlooms Are Worthy of Place

Traditionally, the French reserve their deepest affection for tangible links to caring ancestors who lived centuries apart. For them, cherished *objets d'art,* formal portraits, and a confident blend of furniture—cut from different woods in different eras—thoughtfully handed down generation after generation, offer the reassuring feeling of the familiar while placing a strong claim on the heart.

No matter that these legacies might appear to need some cosmetic help. Signs of time, not painstaking restorations bent on stripping away years, add to their old-world panache. And though more than a few may be somewhat overwhelming for their less roomy, new settings, most are thrust into prominent spots where they garner a certain deference by virtue of their age.

*Enfilade means, literally, "in a row," referring to doors, windows, even rooms aligned in an orderly chain, in keeping with seventeenth-century customs.

Reversible Nancy Corzine harlequin fabric used on one side and then the other turns a humble pantry into a glamorous space. Meanwhile, needlepoint roosters and hens perch in pillows, adding a personal touch. Trim is from Kenneth Meyer Company, San Francisco.

Opposite: In the orderly world of the French, glasses are generally within easy reach. Renovating an antiquated kitchen led to a mosaic of possibilities stateside as well, including cabinets with brass numerals that once opened doors to hotel rooms in France.

Reinforcing the room's strong architecture, Jacques Bouvet et Cie fabrics – available through McRae Hinkley, San Francisco – tumble effortlessly, thanks to the curtain's weighted edges.

Opposite: Marrying old-world architecture to twenty-first-century ease can be a challenge, but tradition reigns in a family room offering deep seating for everyday comfort. Fabric by Jacques Bouvet et Cie covers sofas; the coffee table is from Ironies in Berkeley, California. In the eighteenth century this armoire was built for nobility. Equally impressive is the massive seventeenth-century French limestone fireplace.

Cruiser enjoys his moments in the sun, not burdened by the fact that Louis XVI hated cats!

A detail of a window just steps away from a wine room.

Opposite: Shapely slipcovers skim upholstery, protecting dressmaker stitching – tucks, folds, and inverted pleats – from Cruiser, the much-loved family cat. Eighteenth-century aristocrats often retained attendants to oversee an array of responsibilities, from maintaining upholstery to giving furnishings a fresh look with coverings echoing the season.

There are exceptions, of course, but as a rule, no wood piece receives a greater welcome than the armoire—as well it should. It is, after all, emblematic of French country life, suggestive of a people's aspirations and fears, and likewise, the once symbolic heart of a bride's dowry, elevated above most other material attachments.

Built in thirteenth-century France initially for storing armor, thus heir to the name, armoires soon became fashionable for housing an entire family's clothes and other sparse possessions, since closets were not common in dwellings until the twentieth century. These days, meters of fabric veil rough edges of aging shelves, undercutting their ability to snag seductive linens or reveal the many secrets that they hoard.

Heavily carved or not, the consensus is that looks are not everything. The point of pride confirming value and status is provenance. A document authenticating origin and chronicling previous ownership—including identifying the experts who have vetted the piece in the past—enhances the worth of any antique. But then, even a less-than-captivating armoire of mysterious provenance commands respect when accompanied by airs of eighteenth-century France. However real or imagined such tales may be, each adds immeasurably to the cachet.

At the turn of the nineteenth century, about twenty-six million people lived in France. Although no one tracked the number of towering armoires adorning aristocratic mansions, clearly, over the years, the quantity of prestigious eighteenth-century pieces dwindled. Many dragged out to barricade roads did not survive the ravages of the French Revolution, never mind later wars that took a toll when some *were* literally left out on the street as people moved back into smaller houses once happily left behind.

Since then, Americans have wooed others across the ocean with offers of refashioned images, conforming more to stateside tastes. But our

Opposite: In 1783, the Montgolfier brothers launched a hot air balloon constructed of paper and linen, carrying a cockerel, a sheep, and a duck in its basket. After the first manned flight lifted off from Versailles later that same year, Marie Antoinette declared ballooning "the sport of Gods." Commemorating the event is a powder room upholstered in fabric by the French house Pierre Frey.

A salvaged etched-glass panel – fitted into a door – dating back to nineteenth-century France opens into the dining room.

While reclining on a chair wearing Nomi fabric, a British-made pillow flaunts boundless creativity. Antique velvet boasts a sophisticated applique, topped with net.

Opposite: An artfully fashioned dining room brims with culture and charm, with help from an eighteenth-century fireplace unearthed in Paris. Toile is from Cowtan & Tout. An Asmara carpet anchors the room.

practice of turning yesterday's armoires into dwellings for tidy entertainment centers inevitably leaves the French aghast. Forget sentimentalism or their penchant for hosting electronics in full view. When the ratio of eighteenth-century armoires to those vying for them is so awry, we are doing the unthinkable, critics say. That these pieces are as beloved by Americans as by the French seemingly offers little consolation.

Balance Is Key to Creating a Feeling of Well-Being

There is no denying that integrating boldly scaled, dignified, old wood pieces can be *très difficile,* even for the French. Unless those clamoring for the spotlight find their way to the right places, their presence can jarringly slant the visual weight to one side of a room.

It is not by accident, then, that ancestral portraits pose arrogantly on easels, taut tapestries look down from walls, and folding screens brushed with painted scenes help project an air of authority, say, across the room from statuary. Or that oils, gouaches, and prints swell into collections, stretching toward the horizon. Though none may tote equalizing weight, each helps view attention-grabbing furnishings in a more flattering light. Not that there need be something in every corner basking in an imperial mirror's reflected glow; but striking a proper balance is the secret behind settings with vitality of their own.

Harmony Is More Important than Comformity

The French would no more purchase a bedroom "suite" than a so-called dining room "set" with wood finishes boringly alike. As for lamps, even they tend to be unique. And while Americans may crave five-piece place settings of the same china, our French cousins do not. Most frown on matching sets of anything, preferring, instead, inventive pattern mixes as dinner and bedtime companions. Indeed, in homes that want for nothing, disparate elements, each with its own centuries-long résumé, come together in a sophisticated way.

Much like students at the École des Beaux-Arts, Paris's prestigious national art school ensconced on the rue Bonaparte, chairs of different sizes and ages gather in the same room. Centuries ago, furniture stiffly lined the perimeter of a space. But with conversation now elevated to a learned art, furnishings are amiably grouped to encourage shared confidences and spirited debates over concerns open to general discussion.

Essentially, entertaining requires an equal number of places in the *salon* as in the dining room, so talks can continue even after a lingering meal followed by dessert. For one to simply pick up and leave without engaging in further conversation is considered politically incorrect, as then a dinner party is thought less than successful.

Elegance Must Mingle with Ease

With strong, stately architecture—soaring ceilings, imposing fireplaces, generously chiseled moldings, and exquisite parquet floors—the foundation and framework of French pride, graciously scaled *salons* echo with cherished, avidly collected antiques, faithfully honoring the Republic of France.

Preceding Overleaf, Left: A variety of textiles and textures meet in the living room of this San Francisco home.

Preceding Overleaf, Right: Since 1300, the Italians have been painting furniture that flaunts its charm. Etched, mirrored doors make this handsome nineteenth-century *bibliothèque* (bookcase) especially coveted.

Opposite: Among the wide array of centuries and cultures present in the room is a period Napoleon III *bibliothèque,* wearing its original paint. The important Second Empire piece is from Brian Stringer Antiques, Houston. Leather-bound books and other collectibles add easy elegance.

A nineteenth-century walnut *buffet a deux corps* (cupboard in two parts) from Jacqueline Adams Antiques, Atlanta, showcases prized French silvered glass – a thin, double-walled glass with silver coating within – known also as mercury glass. The collection dating back to the nineteenth century hails from the Paris flea market. Lee Jofa Fabric wraps the buffet's interior.

Preceding Overleaf: The epic scale of this *salon* requires oversized furnishings, starting with the limestone fireplace, or *cheminee,* as it is called in France. A generously sized chandelier of Italian descent hovers over an antique Oushak carpet air-freighted from Turkey to Nouri & Sons, Houston. American-made sofas are from the Cameron Collection at George Cameron Nash, Dallas; pillow fabric is Christopher Hyland, a velvet check. Walnut console backing up to the sofa is from Italy, circa 1690. Accessories, too, are antique.

Opposite: Elsewhere in the room sits an antique stained-glass top – once part of a light fixture in a French hotel – supported by a custom base by Peck & Company, Ironsmiths, Houston. The late-nineteenth-century Louis XV *fauteuils* are from Skelton-White in Houston.

It is not enough, however, for expansive living quarters to brim with precious objects exhibited like museum artifacts. Ultimately, convention dictates, possessions must represent a culture that prizes understatement, which means teaming the unassuming with that more grand—or, if one will, mixing princely furnishings and humble finds.

As a link, the French hand-paint otherwise plain chairs, tables, cabinetry—most everything that began life simply—not to astonish, but for their own pleasure. While they believe in living in beautiful spaces, overly serious rooms do not make sense in many modern homes. Nor do rarely used, untouchable places defined by theater ropes. With pets and families fueling life, it is unpardonable for a room to be reserved solely

for after-dark parties that require crystal flutes of Veuve Clicquot held aloft by handsome waiters no less interesting than the guests.

Instead, settings must serve as family gathering spots, where dogs can wag their tails among a crowd of photos in antique frames, stacks of cherished books, and enough freshly cut, monochromatic flower arrangements to furnish the capital's elegant Plaza Athénée Hôtel. The French adore flowers, believing that one color *en masse* highlights the shape and texture of blooms. But in the view of many, plants belong outdoors on the balcony or terrace.

So, with a practiced air, the precious sit politely near the less-pricey, the ordinary across the room from the extraordinary—each attracting interest now and then, though some finer things, such as *trumeaux* (painted overmantels), *jardinières* (plant containers), and shapely clocks—once symbols of power—do demand more than their fair share of attention. Yet, even when interiors exude glamour few can ignore, there are signs of family life, as if dismissing the commonly held American notion that fine furniture and children do not mix.

Collections Make Settings More Interesting

With their strong sense of self, commanding style, and admirable persistence, the French are collectors second to none. The hunt for antiques, or *la chine,* as they say, is an obsession rooted in desire to preserve France's artistic treasures both for themselves and for their children. But the rush of the chase is also addictive.

Across France, neighborhood *brocantes* (flea markets) abound. Similarly, Saturday *vide-greniers* stir streams of local *habitués* into shopping frenzies, promising all manner of secondhand finds, from the expected to the intriguing to the surprising. Whereas some literally empty their attics casting the all-but-forgotten from their lives, others seemingly cannot be deterred from hauling home Vuitton valises, old brass scales

Preceding Overleaf, Left: A butler's pantry – swathed in Phillip Jeffries wallcovering – provides plenty of storage for glasses above and linens below. While large cracks are not especially desirable in vintage *pots de confit* that once preserved duck or goose for *cassoulet,* a South of France specialty, most collectors expect to see signs of wear. Tile shown here is from Architectural Design Resource, Houston.

Preceding Overleaf, Right: Natural light streams in windows, as if knowing that the kitchen is a family hub. Aside from high-tech appliances, there are perching places for the children at a central island. The palette acts as a go-between for the butler's pantry and a sitting room (unseen), cooling any rivalry.

Opposite: Whether family, friend, or visiting dignitary, houseguests receive the royal treatment in a room draped in a bed from Patina made in Italy – as it has the same presence as the antique that inspired it. Quadrille plumps European pillows; Cowtan & Tout makes up the billowing bed skirt. The night table is nineteenth century.

Venetians created transparent colored glass in a variety of hues, first using the term "crystal" in the fifteenth century. This delicate chandelier is new but reminiscent of vintage fixtures. It is available with rich green candelabra covers – and other colors, too – through Kuhl-Linscomb, a 12,000-square-foot lifestyle shop in Houston.

Opposite: Above the sink hangs a Venetian mirror, which brings more than a trace of glamour into a young girl's bathroom. From Brunschwig & Fils comes the moss wallcovering, a toile. In 1760, when Chistophe-Philippe Oberkampf launched a copperplate-printing factory in Jouy-en-Josas, a village outside Paris, toile applied to the textile, but it soon became synonymous with monochromatic pastoral scenes.

for weighing melons, and enamel kitchenware from the 1920s and 1930s, to say nothing of nickel hinges, copper pots, and other modest bits of daily existence they cannot picture living without.

Indeed, room settings are disarming repositories for an ever-evolving panoply of boxes, porcelain plates, decanters, and candlesticks varying in size and, in many cases, pointing out the obvious: A collection makes the strongest statement when artfully congregated together, rather than scattered around the room.

This is not to imply that objects jostle each other for space on crowded tables, or that rooms stray toward the cluttered. Despite a reputation as collectors, the French are schooled early on in the less-is-more philosophy, which teaches that one liberally scaled treasure can have a greater impact than a sport utility vehicle full of antiques. As a result, most think like Napoléon (1769–1821), who told his followers, "Everything that is big is beautiful."

Moreover, assembling and arranging *objets d'art*—in a seemingly effortless way—is a trait at which people excel. Spaces do not look overly orchestrated. Rather, accessories appear to have offhandedly found their own way to alluring spots. Yet, compositions are indeed the result of careful planning, as the French leave nothing to chance. In truth, their exacting nature is a conviction on which the culture rests.

The master bath floor has as its centerpiece a mosaic. The earliest known mosaics were made in 300 B.C. in Mesopotamia.

Staking a claim to the air space over the master bath is an iron chandelier with wooden beads, a treasured flea-market find of Italian origin.

Opposite: A settee transports a decidedly European flavor to a master bedroom that doubles as a sitting room. The painted table is from the flea market in Parma, Italy.

Key Is Layering Patterns, Textures, and the Lush Palette of France

Mixing hues in ways only nature would dare is a rite of the French. But then, "the logic of nature is impeccable," pointed out Hector Guimard (1867–1942), creator of the impressive cast-iron signs gracing entrances to the Paris Métro.

Faithful to natural pigments, *maisons* echo with the breathtaking blues of the Mediterranean, the balmy sunflower yellows, the glorious poppy reds, and the shifting shades of leafy greens that offer limitless decorating choices. As if this were not enough, settings also coax drifts of color from the earth, such as ochre, sienna, umber, and, not least, terra-cotta.

At first glance, spaces appear uncomplicated, until a closer look reveals how they are composed. Starting with roughly troweled walls, a glaze coat adds depth, imparting a soft, rich surface that reflects light differently than paint. Then, a mix of fabric weaves transforms flat planes into areas three-dimensional as an unexpected interplay of contrasts—matte and shiny, light and dark, sophisticated and relaxed—complement each other.

As it happens, smooth textures communicate a more refined spirit than rough textures, which often attract more attention than deserved. This is because flat surfaces catch the light, exuding a sheen or warmer finish. Think silks, taffetas, and watermarked moirés—all fabrics that gleam and

convey a dressier feeling than, say, textiles such as cottons, twills, and denims, whose warp (vertical) and woof (horizontal) threads cast shadows that mask the light, thus veiling colors and making them appear darker and duller than they are.

Curiously enough, a room with few textures produces the feeling of space. But an intriguing grouping of surfaces and shapes—looking down from walls and up from floors—is considerably more interesting. To keep silhouettes from competing with one another, the French avoid placing two objects the same size side by side. This is not to suggest that shapes do not repeat, only that varied forms—round, rectangular, square, and oval—nestle amongst each other. Beyond that, fabric *always* separates hard surfaces, avoiding rivalry between two wood pieces, known to coexist warily.

Carefully Wrought Details Further Set a Room Apart

The French fastidious attention to detail harks back to the seventeenth century when Louis XIV and his visionary finance minister, Jean-Baptiste Colbert, established a strictly controlled guild system that regulated the work of artisans, holding their specialties to the highest set of principles and making selling outside one's guild punishable.

Ébénistes faced wood pieces with costly ebony veneer, *menuisiers* constructed solid wood furniture from the finest raw materials, *vernisseurs* fashioned lacquer pieces, and *doreurs* highlighted furnishings and architecture with gold leaf, or gilding. Some artisans would become well known; yet, dozens of others, hardly less impressive, lavished skill and attention on the smallest detail of their craft before stamping a piece with their name—a guild requirement—unless made for the royal court; then it carried a palace inventory number.

Preceding Overleaf, Left: Taking advantage of today's creative freedom, an eighteenth-century tapestry of the picturesque French countryside embraces a nineteenth-century Portuguese settee. Across the room stands a table of Italian descent. Also from Italy is an eighteenth-century chandelier whose candles are lit each day at dusk. The far end of the entry boasts a pair of antique Rococo consoles with silver gilding. The floor is reclaimed Salteo – a terra-cotta–colored clay baked in the sun rather than fired in a kiln – found throughout Europe.

Preceding Overleaf, Right: Add the French reverence for history to a passion for fine colored crystal, and you have a disarming mix of old and new that pleases the eye. Mounted on a carved backplate that long ago served Easter mass in one of France's many Catholic churches is an antique sconce. The gilt game table, steeped in history, is Venetian. Bedecking the mirrored niche is French Cristal Saint-Louis from Neiman-Marcus, Dallas.

Opposite: Inspired by their travels to Africa, homeowners led a powder room in a different direction. Plaster walls brushed in oil paints depict various times of day – sunrise is reflected in the mirror.

Opposite: Appreciation for the old, the unusual, the unexpected, and the unique ultimately led to a sitting room that looks far from commonplace. The nineteenth-century chandelier is from Genoa; a French priest's vestment serves as a tablecloth. The crown on the coffee table is also French. The sisal is available from Stark Carpet.

Preceding Overleaf, Left: Embellishing her bathroom is a faithful copy of a Lombary commode, crafted by artisan Louis Bauer, of Fort Worth, Texas. An age-old method called "lost wax" was used in replicating eighteenth-century hardware. Using clay, one takes an impression, then fills the mold with wax before dropping it into a vat of plaster. When fired in a kiln, the wax evaporates, creating a new mold in which bronze – an alloy of copper and tin – is poured.

Preceding Overleaf, Right: Billowing gauze from Great Plains marries delicacy and grandeur, fashioning a *salle de bain* with an old-world feeling. Blackamoors in Oriental wear keep watch over marble mosaic flooring and fittings from Herbeau France, also available at Herbeau Creations of America in Naples, Florida. The dressing room on the back cover is nearby.

Opposite: Transporting old-world elegance while sumptuously dressing the room is an iron bed and bedding, both from Chelsea Textiles. Donna Burley of Straight Stitch Dallas fabricated the soft furnishings.

After the French Revolution, the guild system was abolished and the quality of some early-nineteenth-century workmanship fell. For the most part, however, artisans remained dedicated to producing furnishings with merit. These days, the French maintain a commitment to the decorative arts with help from the *Comité Colbert,* established in 1954. Its mission is to encourage and recognize creative excellence. Among its seventy members are the well-known houses of Baccarat, Bernardaud, and Hermès (the luxury firm famous for its leather), as well as Chanel, Lalique, Louis Vuitton, and D. Porthault (perhaps the most prestigious name in French linens). Current associates must approve prospective members who have met rigid guidelines.

But even less-renowned matters do not escape French minds. Whether replacing door hardware, selecting quality leather for a chair, or hanging art on walls, the attention to minutiae is striking. A spot of leopard used in an imaginative way adds a touch of whimsy without sacrificing a setting's dignity. Curtains with startling linings hang as luxuriously as couture gowns, since it is unthinkable to skimp on fabric. Polished brass grilles with scrolled motifs cover heating vents. Throws artfully wrap sofas. Deep rather than shallow *bullions* (thick, twisted fringes) and other trims communicate style whether viewed up close or from afar. Lights can be up-turned for reading, and perfectly poised tables await newspapers, a glass of wine, or a book—all signature touches that make a space inviting.

In truth, the level of detail in tasteful French rooms is enough to provoke envy. But, then, the Sun King, Madame de Pompadour (Louis XV's beautiful mistress) and Queen Marie Antoinette were, indeed, strong role models, though the French shy away from name-dropping.

Of course, nothing escaped Napoléon's attention either. He redesigned the uniforms of his military, filled his tent with smart mahogany

campaign furniture as well as hundreds of books, and even felt compelled to rename his West Indies–born wife "Josephine" when her given name was Rose. And, yes, he passed a law forbidding married women from buying property without their husbands' consent after Josephine purchased Malmaison—a retreat outside Paris—in 1799 while he was in Egypt. More progressively, perhaps, he streamlined fourteen thousand decrees into seven unified laws applying to all citizens, which more than seventy governments used verbatim or patterned new laws after by 1960.

The point is, more than two hundred years after he died, Napoléon still exerts a powerful influence in France. For people hardly create mindless rooms shaped by chic collectibles. Though few can resist hosting, even for a time, fragments of history with links to another century, decorating, for the French, goes well beyond simply filling their homes with handsome antiques. Shaping the art of living are the values that the French proudly hold dear.

The French headboard is old, while the canopy ring was newly carved to match. Fabric is from Chelsea Textiles, based on an eighteenth-century design. A doorway frames the bathroom beyond.

A detail of bottles from Murano, Italy. Some are old, others new.

Left: A mirrored dressing table steps out of the Art Deco era. But *le table de toilette* actually made its debut late in the seventeenth century. Madame de Pompadour – Louis XV's official mistress, or *maîtresse en titre*, who had extraordinary influence – ceremoniously encouraged courtiers seeking the king's favor to present themselves at an hour when she would be *à la toilette*, aware that she looked especially alluring at that time.

Savoir-
FAIRE

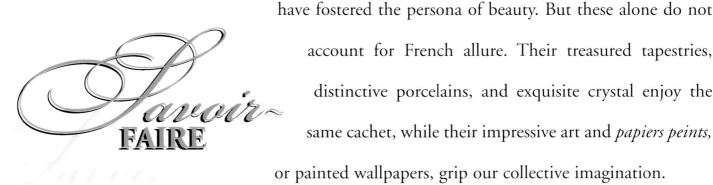

Seducing us with their self-assured approach to design, glamorous culture, and lasting respect for the past, we hold the French in awe, magnifying their presence in the world by elevating them to symbols of taste, splendor, and unshakable stylistic authority. For centuries now, it seems, their fine furniture, regal array of textiles, and embroidered linens have fostered the persona of beauty. But these alone do not account for French allure. Their treasured tapestries, distinctive porcelains, and exquisite crystal enjoy the same cachet, while their impressive art and *papiers peints,* or painted wallpapers, grip our collective imagination.

Seemingly, the influence of the French is everywhere one looks these days. It parades smartly down American fashion runways, graces dining rooms serving fine cuisine, ambles off the drafting boards of architects eager to imprint their visions, and bounds into the studios of top design experts waiting to fill houses with the beautiful and unusual. And even that is far from all. The fact is, no other country exudes the global reach that France has attained, exporting more luxury goods than any other country.

Understandably, then, the *savoir-faire* of the people is deserving of our focus. For the French way of doing things is indeed different from other cultures on the Continent, or more plainly—everyone else.

Preceding Overleaf: A wall of windows invites the outside into a conservatory bedecked in a green-and-white Schumacher toile, plus bamboo. The iron table with glass top is from Niermann-Weeks. Hand-painted pagoda pillow is by Fabulous Things, in Atlanta. Stalks of fresh bamboo fill a basket arranged by Judy Blackman at Blumengarten, Dallas. In Eastern cultures it symbolizes strength, longevity, and good luck. While it takes the average human years to grow four feet, it takes some forms of bamboo only a day.

Opposite: Vintage chairs outfitted in Quatrain, Inc., tailored skirts surround an antique table. The Aubusson rug takes its name from the French city where the carpets were first made.

A detail of architectural engravings – all rooms in an Italian villa.

Right: A tailored banquette at one end of a living room invites dining informally in style. With games back in fashion, it also is the perfect spot to get together for a bridge party. Chairs sport Colefax & Fowler. Wall sconces are from Nicholas Antiques, New York City.

Above: Bouquets of flowers shower the curtain in a young girl's bathroom with charm.

Below: Arthur has yet to use these towels from Restoration Hardware. His wallcovering is from Stroheim & Romann, Inc.

Opposite: A butler's pantry off the breakfast room works as an elegant potting room. The fanciful and functional antique sink hints that spring is near, though it is too early in the year for much other than tulips and hyacinths to flower. Fittings are from Period Brass.

An airy loggia is lined with parrot engravings from Chelsea House in Gastonia, North Carolina.

Opposite: Prettying up a guest bathroom is a hand painted commode from the Roberta Schilling Collection, Atlanta. Fittings are Period Brass. Wallcovering is by Osborne & Little.

Louis XVI chairs upholstered in Kravet tiger chenille bring a playful spirit to a salon reflecting the owner's enviable style – sophisticated, charming, and fun! Neoclassicism was a reaction to Rococo excess in the later half of the eighteenth century, borrowing motifs from ancient Greece and Italy's excavations of Herculaneum (1738) and Pompeii (1748).

Opposite: Against a backdrop of floor-to-ceiling bookshelves, lords, ladies, and ordinary mortals sit as equals just as kings and knights did long ago – with no one feeling left out, or sitting below the salt, as King Arthur once said. The shelves hold antique Chinese porcelain and favorite books.

To create a versatile, multi-use foyer worthy of a sophisticated three-story urban townhouse out a narrow ground floor back hall, add a Venetian settee, Chinoiserie lacquered mirror, and porcelain plates.

Opposite: French doors open to a walled courtyard with antique fountain, offering houseguests more than the comforts of many five-star hotels. Authentically French, toiles de Jouy prints originated in the village of Jouy-en-Josas, near Versailles. Popular during the reigns of Louis XVI and Napoleon, they traveled to the United States after the American Revolution. Fabric and wallcovering from Thibaut envelop the room.

A late-seventeenth-century tapestry from a chapel in France offers a visual feast while serving as a backdrop for an elegant dining room's exquisite china, delicate crystal, and fine linens. Louis XV-style chairs boast their original petit point coverings from the nineteenth century. Sweeping curtains – luxuriously constructed with hidden interlining – wear Lee Jofa fabric. Custom umber glaze is by Joiful Artworks, Vacaville, California.

Table Matters

Given the country's lofty reputation as a gastronomic mecca, it is no surprise that good food accompanied by fine wine and stimulating conversation is a cornerstone of French life.

For many, a trip to *la boulangerie* (bakery) for the country's heralded fresh croissants is a daily ritual. But then again, so is drinking strong coffee and foamy milk from a hand-painted *café au lait* bowl, or slowly enjoying a cup of steaming espresso while reading newspapers from the corner kiosk.

Come lunch, most shops outside central Paris close between noon and two or three o'clock so the staff can indulge at their own gourmet havens, if not in other dependable spots, since *le déjeuner à midi* is the day's most important meal. Most favor lighter fare for dinner, and between-meal snacking is almost unheard of, notwithstanding trips to Ladurée, the Parisian *pâtisserie* rightly famous for the macaroons that often keep American tourists going between meals. For the French, there also is no getting away from Saturday jaunts to the chocolate buffet at Il Palazzo in the Hôtel Normandy near the Louvre.

If wishes could come true, many might hope for Versace china, Wallace sterling silver – and crystal purchased on holiday in Florence and Venice. Gianni Versace layers patterns and colors for Rosenthal, a German company founded in 1897.

Many credit the formidable Catherine de Médici (1519–89), who came to Paris in 1533, at age fourteen, to wed the Duc d'Orléans, the future King Henri II (1519–59), with defining acceptable table manners. Educated in Florentine mores, she brought along an entourage of Italian chefs and pastry cooks, and packed several dozen silver dinner forks in her luggage. Before giving birth to the custom of permitting women to dine at the table with men, she warned that bulging waistlines were distasteful and touted the benefits of wearing corsets to achieve an hourglass figure—which unquestionably has had bearing on every generation since.

Yet it was François Vatel, Prince de Condé's admired "master of the kitchen," who assured France's ascendancy to the pinnacle of culinary fashion in 1671. Hoping to impress King Louis XIV, the Prince planned a glittering three-day *fête* at Château de Chantilly, his magnificent estate twenty-five miles north of Paris that gave Chantilly crème its name. Entertainment included fireworks and water ballet. But when the fish course failed to arrive in time for the final night's banquet, Vatel committed suicide. As the tale goes, "The shame is too much to bear," he wrote, forever linking himself to France's gastronomic history. To say the French have taken dining seriously ever since is equally apt.

Louis XIV was the first French king to offer guests three-piece place settings of a knife, fork, and spoon, though he chose to eat with his fingers throughout his life—perhaps because he considered using these tools unmanly, as some historians suggest. But after bursts of violence where diners attacked and sometimes killed each other at meals, the Sun King outlawed pointed, double-edged daggers at the table and in 1669 ordered that all dinner knives have rounded ends, so dining would be less dangerous.

Later, when his excesses put a drain on France's assets, the king melted all flatware and replaced formal silver hollowware and plates with ceramic pieces, boosting interest in the country's humble *faïence* (tin-glazed earthenware) industry. Though perhaps not an economically sound thing to do, French *faïence* glazes distinguish the ware to this day.

By American standards, French kitchens are efficient but modest, without pricey professional-looking appliances and state-of-the-art cabinets admired for their beauty. Within easy reach, or *sous la main* (meaning "under the hand"), are *la batterie de cuisine*—the copper pots, pans, bowls, and molds—dented from use—that cooks hold dear. For centuries now, master coppersmiths in the small Norman village of Villedieu-les-Poêles have forged gleaming cookware.

Formal, seated dinners have all the requisite garnishes of fine dining: attractive linen cloths that sweep the floor, resplendent mixes of fine china, polished silver flatware and heirloom candelabras, plus sparkling crystal. In contrast to other cultures, the French set their table with the fork tines facing down, a custom

A salvageable fragment of an eighteenth-century painting that met with misfortune graces a nineteenth-century painted *enfilade* in the foyer. (During the French Revolution, tapestries also were cut into pieces.) From Parma, Italy – where dealers serve as guiding lights for making Italian rooms look Italian – come the nineteenth-century altar sticks.

A Portola Valley, California, living room has the makings of a Right Bank *salon:* A pair of mirrors (one unseen), a miniature sedan that formerly held small treasures, and a hand-carved capital (head of a column or pillar), now a table – all with origins in eighteenth-century France. Seventeenth-century textiles make up the pillows. Inspiration for the palette came from an Agra carpet, woven in India. The experts at Christie's auction house say a carpet measures nine feet by six feet or more, while rugs are smaller, though we commonly use the terms interchangeably.

that developed because someone thought fork-tines-up looked too aggressive. At the same time, tines facing down draw attention to engraved initials or the decorative motifs, intended to be noticed without being obvious.

On occasions when only the best will do, many Parisians rely on star floral designer Christian Tortu in the Sixth Arrondissement for party-perfect centerpieces that do not interfere with conversations. Astonishing edible sculptures—temples, fountains, hedges, and large baskets with spun flowers of every description—fashioned from sugar paste were once a creative option. Then the Sèvres porcelain factory developed *biscuit*—unglazed white porcelain closely resembling sugar paste—thus replacing the fragile confections that rivaled for attention on tables across the Continent.

More often than not, *le tout Paris* ships soiled table linens to Marie Lavande, the exquisite old-fashioned laundry. Here, attendants in white coats use heavy flatirons to fastidiously incorporate creases, not erase them, thereby reviving the grand seventeenth-century art of breaking and folding before returning the wash beautifully packaged in a manner that fits one's shelves.

When dining *en famille,* Parisians pay equal attention to detail, but take a more relaxed approach. The table is set with a handsome cloth that may cascade to the floor, pottery, heavy flatware, and perhaps chunky bubble-filled glassware made in the village of Biot. Knife rests infuse mealtime with a sense of occasion, together with armfuls of flowers that come straight from painterly gardens or flower stands at nearby Métro stops. The secret behind creating beautiful round bouquets is stripping away most foliage and arranging stems diagonally in a spiral.

When it comes to table settings, it is rare to see the same pattern used throughout the meal. Whether fine china or *faïence,* mismatched services add a certain flair. There is an expression: *bien composé,* meaning well composed . . . easily translated yet it cannot be easily explained. Like nearly all things in France, it is a question of taste.

For most, cuisine is far more than merely a way to satisfy hunger; it is a theatrical production with all the trappings of a Broadway show, meaning it's inventively propped, perfectly staged, and, most importantly, carefully scripted to defy expectations as much because of the presentation as the fare. While specialties *de maison* vary with seasonal loyalty to regionally produced ingredients, the unspoken rules governing dinner parties, for the most part, remain unchanged.

Typically, the French invite six, ten, fourteen, or eighteen guests—not eight, twelve or sixteen—assuring that men and women alternate on either side of the hosts, who sit facing each other at the center of the table. It is a *faux pas* to separate engaged couples or those married less than a year.

Furthermore, it is not proper to offer a second helping of soup or even salad and cheese or fruit, which are served after the main course. Nor is it correct to serve champagne with dessert, unless it accompanies each course of the meal. Finally, at smart dinner parties, coffee is always served in the *salon,* since most, quite naturally, have one.

Like other civilizations, the culture has soul hidden in its cuisine, something that is not always easy for outsiders to see, especially since the French are most private and generally only invite relatives and close friends into their homes.

While it is ideal to learn to cook from a native, there is no need to spend a lifetime learning to conjugate French verbs before enrolling in one of Paris's many cooking classes; many are taught in English. At Françoise Meunier's Cooking Classes, one learns to prepare regional specialties, while Frédérique Lauwerier's Diet Café teaches how to prepare light, healthy meals exhibiting more restraint. Within the swank Hôtel Ritz is also a five-star program.

An ancient goddess that once guarded a villa in France waits to be uncrated and contribute to a San Francisco garden's spellbinding look.

Opposite: Elsewhere in the living room on page 104, religious figures from the eighteenth and nineteenth centuries unite faith and art. They rest on an important eighteenth-century commode from the Piemonte region of Italy that borders France. In place of a painting hangs a collection of vintage textiles known as *ex voto,* Latin for "from a vow." The embroidered gilt letters – "G" and "R" – centered on the cloth, give thanks for divine favors, or grace received. As furniture built for nobility, chairs are gilded. They flaunt Nomi fabric, hand-painted with gold.

In seventeenth-century France, *chinoiserie* became the rage, so it makes perfect sense that it would be called upon to swathe a French dining room in glamour. The Directoire-style (1789–1804) table is solid mahogany. The Venetian chairs replicate ones found in the eighteenth century with paint and gold finish. Window treatment fabric is Coraggio edged in Ellen Holt; embroidered detailing further sets the curtains apart. Jeffrey Lee at Urban Flower in Stanley Korshak, Dallas, designed the bouquets.

Le Chocolat

An uplifting goblet of hot chocolate—with whipped cream on the side—has long been a great attraction. It is what drew novelist Marcel Proust, legendary fashion icon Coco Chanel, and millions of tourists before and after them to the famously resplendent Café Angélina, with its marble-topped tables, gilt-framed murals, and Napoléon III columns, on rue de Rivoli, near the Jardin des Tuileries.

In the beginning, *tchocolati* was a bitter beverage drunk by the Mayas and the Aztecs in Mexico. The Spanish explorer Hernán Cortéz introduced the drink, sweetened with cane sugar, to Europe in 1520. Anne of Austria, a Spanish princess who would wed the future King Louis XIII, then

A Royal Worcester porcelain coffee pot isn't exactly a chocolate pot but does serve the purpose. The homeowner inherited the sterling tray from his grandmother.

introduced chocolate to France nearly a century later. Once she became queen, she declared chocolate *the* drink of the royal court.

Rooted in South and Central America, chocolate (in Greek, meaning "food of Gods") comes from cocoa beans, seeds from beans that grow atop *Theobroma,* the cacao tree. Various properties make it energizing. But it is also credited with being an aphrodisiac and an antidepressant since it contains phenyl ethylamine, which has psycho-stimulant properties, and neurotransmitter serotonin.

Following her predecessor's example, Marie-Thérèse of Austria, Louis XIV's wife, caused quite a stir when she proclaimed she had merely two passions: the king and chocolate, thus prompting the Sun King to install at the Palace a "Royal Chocolate Maker to the King," who served the beverage in *chocolatières* (chocolate pots) fashioned from copper, pewter, silver, porcelain, and gleaming gold vermeil.

Most pots had hinged lids, though some had a hinged flap in the lid or else a removable finial, so that a *molinet* (a long wooden whisk) could be inserted into the pot. This was essential because early hot chocolate drinks tended to separate and settle at the bottom. The pear-shaped *chocolatière,* however, allowed space for whisking the chocolate into the desired frothy drink, which was then poured into tall, slender porcelain cups.

During the eighteenth century, the wealthy often commissioned exquisite silver or porcelain chocolate services that included the pot, *molinet,* and cups and saucers. Reportedly, Madame Pompadour, Louis XV's official mistress, ordered the most expensive chocolate service ever produced in France. By then, milk had replaced water—or beer or mulled wine—as the preferred liquid to use in making hot chocolate.

Queen Marie Antoinette, wife of Louis XVI, grew up on the drink in Vienna, and as a result, her royal household also included a chocolate specialist. He sometimes mixed chocolate with powdered orchid bulbs or orange blossoms for her breakfast.

When a new nineteenth-century process made it unnecessary to stir and beat the chocolate, *chocolatières* and *molinets* became obsolete. Nowadays, they are highly collectible.

Eminently fitted to grace the master bedroom is a custom bed that invites admiration. It is impeccably dressed in Brunschwig & Fils and vintage Fortuny, from the elegant Italian fabric company.

Who wouldn't long to hold court in this regal retreat? During the eighteenth century, the *lit d'alcove* made its debut. Being that it parked parallel to a wall, it was also known as *lit de travers*. Crewel-embroidered fabrics were as prized in Georgian times as they are now.

Resting Places

No different than in the time of the ancient Egyptians, beds were the ultimate symbols of wealth in Renaissance Europe. But they were the province of the upholsterer rather than of the furniture maker, since carved frames were rare. By today's standards, beds were also rather short, mostly because people customarily slept at a forty-five degree angle.

When Louis XIV was king, there were no box springs. Instead, plank platforms supported mattresses stuffed with straw, leaves, and pine needles. Heavy, theatrical bed hangings hid plain bedposts, giving carte blanche to the Sun King's famous passionate nature while offering shelter from the cold. The elaborate tapestries or brocades with embroidery-like raised motifs also fixed a bed's worth.

As if exhibiting proof of his unassailable affluence and authority, Louis XIV relished receiving guests from the comfort of his bed. Reportedly, he owned more than four hundred resting places from which he conducted affairs of state. (Most splendid was the *lit de justice*, whose name came to be synonymous with a meeting of parliament in the presence of the king, or a royal edict by the king.)

In keeping with royal whims, the court dismantled these prized possessions and moved them with the seasons from one sumptuous domicile to the next, installing the collection wherever the king and his admirers went. For the bed was more than a piece of furniture from which Louis XIV's grandiose dreams unfolded once he slipped off his hose, removed his red high-heels and then ceremoniously settled down for the night. Each served an explicit intention: birthing heirs (to guard against imposters assuming the throne, the queen was compelled to give birth in public), performing rituals, receiving privileged acquaintances, even dying.

As the king's taste for extravagance and ease spread beyond court circles, rivalry for matchless levels of splendor fueled an array of variations where one could toss and turn. Some suited majestic mansions; others were built for princely places where life was lived a bit more modestly than at Versailles. But all offered discreet protection from drafts, unwelcome guests, and servants' wandering eyes.

Opulently garbed *chambres* (bedrooms) with richly carved headboards were meant to look imposing as the eighteenth century began. By mid-century the *lit d'alcove* (*lit* being the French word for bed) and the *lit à duchesse* replaced humble sleeping spots of years past. Meanwhile, in Brittany, one of the chillier provinces in France, the *lit clos,* hemmed by sliding doors or a mix of doors and fluid curtains, might well have given rise to the expression "sleep tight, don't let the bed bugs bite," though more say "sleep tight" most likely originated when ropes pulled tight kept mattresses from sagging.

Regardless, birds flying arrogantly through open windows and down chimneys presented problems more monumental. As a result, few furnishings were more prized than *ciels* and *baldaquins*—the canopies that both created a grand effect and protected one from the droppings of feathered friends.

Like the Sun King, both Louis XV and Louis XVI had an inventory of ornate beds, from which each made critical decisions, planned hunting parties, and discussed the politics and rivalries of court life, until the storming of the Bastille, when the middle s swept away the monarchy's power, making it ible for many people to live as fashionably as pper class.

the turmoil that followed the French n, it is not surprising that Napoléon once e bed has become a place of luxury for

A detail of a twin hand-painted French bed.

A detail of a young girl's towels in a bathroom that is a world unto itself. According to Porthault, the renowned French linen house, one of the earliest orders for monogrammed linens came from Charles V in 1380.

Opposite: ". . . such stuff as dreams are made on," Shakespeare once said, as if he'd laid eyes on these nineteenth-century hand-painted beds. Like all grandiose appointments, they have a tale of their own. As the teen's paternal great-grandfather purchased them, along with the night table, in France for his five-year-old daughter, her paternal grandmother. Her maternal grandmother transformed the chocolate pot into a lamp. Chair and ottoman are upholstered in Manuel Canovas. The carpet is a handmade Portuguese needlepoint.

While taking its cue from a professional kitchen with high-tech appliances and pot filler mounted on the range wall, this space hosts old-world tradition. Copper pans sway conveniently from a pot rack ready to satisfy an appetite for *mousse au chocolat* or an apple tart.

Opposite: Weather-resistant fabrics settle in a sunny pool house suited to the good life.

Potters from Faenza, Italy, brought to seventeenth-century France a talent for making majolica (or *barbotine,* in French) – earthenware glazed with opaque colors. Villagers in Moustiers and Apt called it *faïence,* though the technique for producing it was identical. The industry grew when the Sun King decreed that the public send all silver and gold to the treasury to pay war debts.

Opposite: This chef enjoys preparing healthy meals and fostering eating habits meant to last a lifetime. Unlike Americans, the French drench most everything in *beurre,* or butter.

me," echoing the prevailing sentiment of many. He then added, "I would not exchange it for all the thrones in the world." At Malmaison, he slept in an Empire (pronounced ahm-peer, on the Continent) bed that sided a wall with wafting fabrics, creating a personal tented retreat fitting an officer. The Empress Josephine's suite held a mahogany swan bed ornamented with gilded bronze upon which she could rest her head.

Few beds with links to eighteenth- and nineteenth-century France survived, and those that endured require odd-sized mattresses. Yet, several distinctively French beds inspired by the originals are still winning praise. Following is a crib sheet to help in sorting out some differences among those laying claim to modern comforts—though several serve specific purposes:

Lit à baldaquin: A canopied four-poster bed.

Lit à colonnes: A four-poster bed.

Lit à la duchesse: A bed dating back to the era of Louis XIV—soon known as "*la duchesse,*" boasting a large, dramatically draped canopy but not bedposts. By the Régence period (1700–30) headboards and footboards emerged, some of like size, others with lower footboards.

Lit à la française: A late-eighteenth-century bed with draped canopy hovering overhead. At first, placed perpendicular to the wall; later, placed lengthwise against a wall.

Lit à la polonaise: A bed swathed in sumptuous fabrics flowing from a large, pointed crown, or tester (from the French *testière,* meaning "headpiece"). *Ciel de lit* is French for a bed tester or canopy, too. In the late eighteenth century, a headboard, footboard, and four bedposts supported an arched iron frame.

A detail of the retractable headboard, bidding goodbye to the day.

Opposite: Plying a master bedroom with style is a custom bed collaboratively designed by the homeowner and architect after the former found the panels incorporated in the footboard. Antique Aubusson fragments dress some pillows, while others wear Bennison Fabrics.

Another view of the master bedroom. Hidden behind the oil painting is a plasma-screen television.

Lit à quenouilles: A distaff bed with four posts supporting an impressive crown.

Lit à travers: A bed or sofa bed placed sideways against a wall, without a canopy. Also known as a *lit d'alcove.*

Lit canapé: A sofa bed backed against a wall, facing into the room, with curtains tumbling from a centered crown.

Lit clos: A bed with sliding wood panels enclosing the sleeping area, or a mix of sliding doors and curtains to ward off late-day chill. During the seventeenth and eighteen centuries, most sided a wall in country estates.

Lit conjugal: Marriage bed.

Lit d'alcove: Also known as a *lit à travers.* A bed or sofa bed placed sideways against a wall, without a canopy.

Lit d'ange: An "angel bed" with a small *ciel,* or canopy, floating over the bed but without bedposts. During the reign of Louis XIV, *noeuds gallants,* or gallant knots, held the curtains in place.

Lit d'enfant: Cot.

Lit gigogne: Pullout bed.

Lit de camp: Camp bed.

Lit de fer: Iron bed.

Lit de parade: Bed of state.

Lit de mort: Deathbed.

Lit de repos: A daybed that commonly functioned as a chair, introduced during the reign of Louis XIII (1610–43) as a perfect place for lounging or napping.

Lit de repos à crosse: A daybed with ends scrolling outward.

Lit en bateau: A nineteenth-century, boat-shaped bed, not unlike the sleigh bed, arched at one end like a ship's prow.

Lits jumeaux: French for twin beds.

Lit pliant or *Lit-cage:* Folding bed.

Lits superposés: Bunk beds.

Above: With an old-world feel that delights the eye, a powder room appears exceptionally smart.

Below: While powder rooms have become luxurious, so have the curtains draping them. Fabric is from Coraggio, the trim is by Passementerie. Wallcovering is by Fonthill.

Opposite: A master sitting room's serene lake view makes for the perfect place to relax and recharge. Bennison Fabrics cover upholstery and dress windows. The rug is sisal.

Hanging art is a balancing act, but the pastoral scene exhibited here also makes a decorative statement. Fabric from Decorators Walk camouflages the wall, while a nubby textile from Kravet sprawls across the bed. Paisleys originated in ancient Babylon.

Opposite: A cozy library is an ideal retreat from the high-tech world. Fabric covering club chair is from Ralph Lauren.

Like a number of furnishings in his house, this bed holds special significance for the designer, as it is where he grew up sleeping back in the sixties after his mother brought it home from a church sale on top of her car. Black-and-white stripe is from Schumacher; the bedcover fabric from Decorator's Walk, and the Greek key from Clarence House. Together they set the proper stage for the architectural renderings.

Not afraid to make a statement in the place he calls home, Chicago designer Tony Stavish mixes flea-market treasures with newer pieces, carving a mellow space for himself. The map of Paris proper is from the Louvre gift shop; the seagrass carpet offers a serene backdrop for more daring objects, including the mercury glass. Sofa is upholstered in a Pindler & Pindler fabric.

In most kitchens, bugs are banned. Here, a generous sampling on cabinet doors helps the space go from plain to a little fancier – as befits a French country kitchen in America. Both the bug prints and the tray are from Pariscope Antiques in Geneva, Illinois. In sixteenth-century French convents, nuns carefully hand-painted humble tin and metal trays, boxes, and lamps, lifting them to an art soon known as *tole*. Alabaster lamp is from Wallner Antiques, Chicago.

A detail shows inexpensive field tile used with more princely priced decorative tile to great effect. Poseidon figurative tile is from Fine Line in Chicago.

Romantic lace curtains grace many windows in France, providing privacy while filtering the light. The town of Calais, on the shores of the North Sea, is the lace capital. Chantilly and Valenciennes are also famous centers.

Fine Linens

Fine linens were once the domain of the rich and noble. Befitting the snobbery of Louis XIV's court, protocol dictated on which type sheeting—pure linen, a mix of linen and cotton, or pure cotton—one would sprawl. But no longer. Now, upstairs/downstairs class differences aside, like-minded Europeans insist on proper linens at every level, suiting the rhythms of daily life—sleeping, bathing, and eating. In fact, across France, Italy, and Great Britain, people begin assembling an assortment of tabletop and bed linens for a baby girl's *trousseau* the moment she is born.

For them, there are no hard-and-fast rules for bed linens to qualify as sensual, but the most elegant ones do share some qualities that set them apart. Most are white or ecru, and more attainable than one might think, although some are more than modestly priced, of course. But other than being 100 percent linen, which becomes softer and whiter with age, or posh Egyptian cotton, the French are not hampered by thread count, which they say can be misleading.

There is a difference, naturally, between 120 and soft 280 or 340 threads per inch, but beyond that, they insist thread count does not really matter, so in Europe, rarely is it mentioned. Instead, there is a consciousness of how linens feel, the comfort they offer, plus additional trappings of splendor—embroidery, appliqué, and applied laces. Those not inclined to compromise their standards covet a soft finishing process.

France has its own bed culture that pays other parts of the Continent little mind. Topping the mattress is a stuffed and quilted mattress pad, followed by two flat sheets, then a blanket that for appearance's sake would not dare to go bare, so another sheet leaves it less exposed. A plump goose-down duvet crowned with a *traversin*—a long, firm, round bolster spanning the bed's width—covered by the bottom sheet before the latter is tucked in, supplies the final layer. Meanwhile, the top sheet—the middle sheet—generously turned back reveals a monogram or the family crest.

In Provence, antique *boutis* (embroidered quilts) pass from one generation to the next. Unlike American quilts that are pieced from leftover scraps, two large pieces of cloth, hand-sewn together and then filled with

batting, make up *boutis* bed covers. In eighteenth-
and nineteenth-century France, women often hand-
stitched motifs inspired by the land—sunflowers,
lavender, olives, and artichokes—on *boutis*.
Nowadays, new coverlets are wished-for gifts in
families not blessed with inherited ones. The
petassoun, or small lap quilt, is commonly fashioned
as a christening present—by descendants of those
who have passed down the art—celebrating new life.

In chic bathrooms, where color is a rarity, thick,
gently scented bath sheets, hand towels, and mitts
jostle for space on gleaming heated rails, waiting to
be called into service. Nearby are *tissanes pour le
bain,* or bath herbs, in tiny cheesecloth sachets,
along with cakes of delicate soap, often made from
formulas dating back centuries. The firm Roger et
Gallet was the official supplier to Napoléon III. But
tried and true Marseille soap is another mainstay to
which many have long clung. Whether green or
white, the weight in grams is stamped on the face
of each piece, as it was centuries ago when

Steeped in tradition yet smartly modern, is a monogrammed blanket
cover from Leontine Linens in New Orleans. A mix of fabrics from
Hinson, Old World Weavers, and Bergamo make up the bed.

Opposite: Putting a faintly forties spin on conventional French is
a settee clad in J. Robert Scott. The clean lines of an Adele Kerr,
Dallas, bed also suit the look. Randolph & Hein, San Francisco,
shipped fabric for the shirred curtains. Animal print is from Travers,
Inc., New York. Brunschwig & Fils crystal lamps embellish custom
side tables. The chandelier is antique.

households kept careful inventories. Since 1688, French law has decreed that only soap made according to
time-honored methods using the purest ingredients can be marked "Savon de Marseille."

Although glimmers of differing regional rituals appear, every terra-cotta-tiled kitchen has an unassuming
porte-torchon, or dish towel holder, attached to the sink wall. With the French flair for detail, easy-to-access
torchons, or dish towels, hang neatly in rows from hooks clearly labeled *mains* (hands), *verres* (glasses),
vaiselles (dishes), and *couteaux* (knives). Coarse fabrics work for knives, pots, and pans, while lint-free linen
helps glassware sparkle, and *métis,* a linen-cotton blend, dries dishes. Collectors covet all of them. But most
popular are red-and-white-patterned *torchons* and those with cross-stitched red monograms embroidered in
the nineteenth century.

The care of linens, unsurprisingly, is something of an art in France. Once women clustered in public washhouses called *lavoirs*, gossiping and sharing news while doing the laundry in gently flowing streams. Afterwards, they dried the wash on the dewy grasses of rambling fields. Legendary for their brilliant whitening powers are the bleaching fields in Flanders—modern-day Belgium. Centuries later, the French still prefer drying linens in the sun rather than in a dryer; however, nowadays they sprinkle laundry with flower-scented waters such as lavender, orange, or jasmine before hand-ironing.

With an uncluttered European hotel look, this bathroom exudes cool efficiency. Sink fixtures are from Pegler, England. Wallcovering is by Schumacher. Wood is mahogany.

A kitchen simmers with style, thanks to finishes selected for warmth and wearability. Prized copper pots, admirable tile, and a commercial range bring the inherent charm of the French countryside.

Nineteenth-century plaster friezes hang above a sofa. All accessories, including the unpretentious silver trays, are old.

A made-in-America hand-painted demilune – meaning "half moon" – console sits amid two well-dressed American-made chairs. Fragments of Fortuny unearthed at the Paris flea market translated into the sophisticated pillows. On the wall hangs an eighteenth-century French mirror flanked by Flemish carved door panels from the same era.

Shedding Some Light

Until the nineteenth century, cooks produced regional meals without the help of La Cornue—the ultimate gourmet range—over roaring fires that also banished the cold and illuminated the homes. For the most part, men and women relished life's simple pleasures. But inside the Palace of Versailles, Louis XIV's appetite for glamour and glitz appeared insatiable.

Thousands of candles helped light the palatial *château* for lavish after-dark *fêtes,* publicizing the Sun King's hunger for excess, to say nothing of his obsession with gold, which he did not take pains to hide. At the same time, they detracted from his support of the decorative arts, which would move royal courts across Europe, beyond the widespread influence of Italy.

Putting on the most dazzling show, light bounced off marble that gleamed and played on furniture polished to a military sheen. In concert, diamonds danced their way into the *Galerie des Glaces,* or Hall of Mirrors, which multiplied the flickering flames, as well as the images of those aristocrats eager to maintain their place in society by staying in the king's favor. Among those adding glitter to gatherings were some who emulated his extravagances, even when beyond their reach.

This is not to say that all that glittered was gold. As if begging to be noticed, solid silver furniture fashioned by the great Jean Bérain lent the castle further elegance. Until 1689, that is, when melted at the Mint of France and converted to coins to help pay the self-indulgent king's exorbitant bills, which, quite naturally, reflected his expensive tastes. To be fair, however, France also required money to help fund the country's armies and seemingly endless wars, which thwarted Louis's ambitions, exhausted the nation, impoverished the people, and laid the foundation for the French Revolution in 1789.

At the turn of the eighteenth century, Paris was growing rapidly. Light streamed through tall windows and French doors, spilling onto oak *parquet de Versailles* floors of newly constructed *hôtels particuliers*, each with a distinctive character but without electricity. When night fell, candles cast a soft glow across dining rooms where guests, seated on damask-upholstered chairs, watched the moon splash in mirrors topped with paintings called *trumeaux,* fitted snugly into *boiserie,* or exquisitely carved paneling.

Opposite: Architectural and garden antiques fill Château Domingue in Houston. Mantels date back to fifteenth-century France, but the 5,000-square-foot warehouse also shelters sixteenth-century fountains, reclaimed flooring, lighting, and doors – some from Italian villas.

Rock-crystal chandeliers, drifting overhead and in mazes of stairs, generated further light, as the wealthy had several per room. (Not until the advent of electricity did the single central fixture become fashionable.) But only the *very* rich could afford odor-free, smokeless beeswax candles. Even smoky tallow candles, made from animal fat, were costly, and were locked away during the day for safekeeping and brought out when needed.

During the reign of Napoléon III (1852–70), often spoken of as the Second Empire, gaslights became a primary source of light after Napoléon III, the nephew of Napoléon Bonaparte, hired Georges-Eugène Haussmann (1809–91) in 1853 to oversee the redevelopment and restoration of Paris, stone by stone.

Driven as the latter was by an obsession to protect France from rebels fighting from the cover of barricades in narrow, twisting streets, Haussmann created broad, arrow-straight boulevards, some decked with opulent stone fountains, all lined with trees. He then lighted the streets and new buildings with 15,000 modern gaslights.

If the stories that abound are to be believed, Empress Eugénie, the glamorous wife of Napoléon III, selected fabric swatches for her fashionable Charles Frederick Worth evening gowns to harmonize with the spark generated by the new streetlights. (Worth [1825–95] was the first couturier to introduce new designs each season, as well as put labels with his name in dresses, thus prompting the fashion system from which our own has evolved.)

At the same time, French Impressionist Pierre-Auguste Renoir (1841–1919) struggled to capture the capital's elusive, changing light *en plein air.* In his famous *Bal du Moulin de la Galette*—finished in 1876 and ultimately bound for the Musée d'Orsay, a former train station—chic Parisians crowd onto the dance floor of an open-air Montmartre café, in the shadow of gaslights resembling luminous white pearls. The charcoal black streetlights in *Rue Cortot en Montmartre,* completed the same year, look much like those that still keep watch over the American Embassy and consulate buildings, as well as the elegant Hôtel de Crillon with its impressive neoclassical façade, sited just off the place de la Concorde. It was here that the Treaty of Paris recognizing the independence of the United States was signed on February 6, 1778, a decade before the building was sold to the Count de Crillon.

Opposite: Tying the past to the present, a *faïence* rooster – symbolic of the people of France – perches on a keystone culled from a shop on rue du Faubourg Saint-Honore in Paris. Rivaling the charm of the countryside, hand-painted tiles – designed by the homeowner and painted by a French artist – frame the stove. Manhattan's Karen Linder added off-hand glamour by painting walls while a rare collection of D'Moiselle d' Avignon (that is "ladies") looked on from the center island. Serving as the chandelier is an old pool table fixture found in Boston.

Several of the artist's bold paintings hang on the wall as tubes of paint, dozens of brushes, and easels nestle in an atelier, surrounded by towering redwoods in the San Francisco hills. Captivated by saturated colors and warm sunlight in the South of France, Vincent Van Gogh (1853–90) became the most intense colorist of his times. His *Sunflowers* sold for $45 million at Christie's auction house in 1987. *Iris* was purchased for $65 million the same year.

Drenched in early morning light, a footed vintage tub wears its original paint while bathing in color. Cast-iron tubs not only last for decades but also retain heat well. The bath sheet is from Hermès, Paris (pronounced air-MEZ, with emphasis on the second syllable).

While affectionately called the City of Light, Paris sits at the same latitude as Montreal and has the same propensity for gray winters and early nightfalls, though it is fair to assume both cities favor touting their beauty. Beyond that, electricity is expensive in France. Therefore, people light their homes with care. As it is, Parisians have a way of capturing light so that it creates a romantic ambience. The key is in the layering of candles, sconces (initially wall brackets with mirror backs and crystal pendants that reflected candlelight), picture lights, and prudently placed table and floor lamps with low wattage bulbs that can be turned up for reading.

Most find that too many lamp shades are distracting; yet they shun track lighting, believing it can be jarring as well as cast unforgiving shadows on the face. In fact, most any overhead light source reduces intimacy, they say. Further, one size picture light does not fit all; the size light depends on the image, not the frame. And fragile textiles are never illuminated.

In the sixteenth century, ancient systems of pulleys and weights raised and lowered hanging fixtures, facilitating lighting and extinguishing candles.

A *salon* exudes Parisian panache – not to mention eighteenth-century elegance – with a towering armoire from Nimes, an impressive French tapestry, beautiful *canapé* and chairs, and early antiques. A rare mid-nineteenth-century Persian Mahal Sultanabad rug adds to the drama.

Today, chandeliers made of glass, wood, or wrought iron create a mood with the aid of dimmer switches. Many alabaster fixtures mirror nineteenth-century gaslights.

Separately, on American shores, people often wonder how to establish size chandelier needed. One accepted maxim says: To determine an appropriate size, add the length and width of the room, then change the word *feet* to *inches.* For example, if the room measures sixteen feet long and fourteen feet wide, hang a chandelier that is approximately thirty inches in diameter. Another school of thought suggests measuring the width of the room, doubling it, and then, again, converting this number to inches for the correct diameter, in this case, twenty-eight inches. Either way, the chandelier will look as if it belongs in the setting, while the wrong size will detract from an enviable effect.

With form and function famously intertwined, the *bouillotte* lamp with multiple candlestick arms set into a brass base—designed for playing a card game by the same name, a precursor to poker—made its debut during the reign of Louis XVI. The table lamp's dish-shaped base held game tokens. As its candles burned, the shade could be lowered to shield players' eyes from glare. Eventually, hollow candle sleeves hid electric wiring.

These days, the French often convert antiques into lamps with the proper shade making each unique. As it turns out, most feel that a round base looks best with a round shade, a square base with a square shade, and a rectangular base with a rectangular shade. Shapes open to interpretation require ingenuity, so most find it best to take the lamp along on a hunt for a shade.

Experts here in the States say the height of a shade should be one-third to one-half the total height of the lamp while the bottom width should be one-half to three-quarters the height of the lamp. The *Paris Exposition des Arts Decoratifs Modernes* of 1925 introduced the standing *torchère,* a floor lamp, which, of course, does not require a shade.

Opposite: A table from Therien, San Francisco, rimmed with Minton-Spidell chairs, graces an elegant dining room that opens to the foyer. Floors are limestone. Window-treatment fabric is from Jim Thompson Silks, with trim by Leslie Hannon. Pair of eighteenth-century screens (unseen) from Le Louvre, Dallas, adorn walls.

From the Old French for "throat" comes the word *gargoyle* – a rainspout decoratively carved in the shape of an imaginary and often grotesque animal through whose mouth rainwater gently streams away from castle walls. This gargoyle is original to the house built in 1880 as a breeding farm for one of the partners in the Comstock Lode, which fueled the development of San Francisco.

Opposite: When dining out means entertaining alfresco, a space spilling onto the terrace can readily suggest the comfortable lifestyle of Provence – especially if saturated colors echo the surrounding landscape. Portuguese and Dutch traders introduced brightly printed *indiennes* to the French in the seventeenth century. For years, the Provencale mini-flowers, more ample flower patterns, and paisleys created such rivalry for the silk and wool textile mills owned by the Crown that they were banned in French provinces.

French CLASS

French CLASS

For centuries, the kings and queens of France lived in magnificent palaces, seemingly indifferent to the sufferings of commoners. But by the eve of the revolution, cries were heard from all factions of society aspiring for better lives. Nobles begrudged the monarchy for stripping power from them, the bourgeoisie resented the privileges of nobility, and the bourgeoisie and the peasants criticized a system where nobility was exempt from taxes while they were not, as well as a structure where only the well-to-do could hold positions of importance, such as that of army officers.

On July 14, 1789, bands of men and women marched through Paris streets chanting, *"Liberté, égalité, fraternité!"* Thousands then stormed the massive Bastille, freeing prisoners, killing the jail's governor, and ushering in a ten-year Reign of Terror—starring a guillotine stationed in the center of Paris. Not satisfied with merely demolishing the Bastille and killing French leaders, the revolutionaries also destroyed other reviled symbols of royalty: buildings, churches, palaces, and statuary.

In the decade that followed the Revolution, Napoléon I longed to restructure the city, starting with construction of the Arc de Triomphe. But he ruled (1804–15) with a harshness that stirred haunting memories. When forced into exile, he abdicated in favor of his only legitimate son, Napoléon II, who never actually governed.

Louis Napoléon Bonaparte III, nephew of Napoléon I, was elected president of France in 1848 and after a *coup d'état* became emperor from 1852 to 1870; his reign is known as the Second Empire. He was determined to metamorphose Paris—from an unstable capital where living conditions were so bad that residents often felt there was no choice but to revolt, into the most elegant imperial city on earth. It made sense, therefore, that he turned to Georges-Eugène Haussmann,

Moldings echo the ceremonial scale and proportions of the master bedroom, with elements lifted from the mirror. J. P. Weaver Company, in Glendale, California, re-creates period interiors.

Koplavitch & Zimmer pearls add luxury to her bathroom curtains, lined and interlined.

Prefect of the Seine, who had twenty-two years experience updating roads and schools in various provinces of the country.

Haussmann would take the city that inspired author Victor Hugo's *Les Misérables*—a dirty, disease-ridden, dangerous, and crowded metropolis fundamentally unchanged since the Middle Ages, unlike the French city fixed in imaginations—and create the Paris beloved today.

Leading an army of 14,000 laborers while borrowing ideas from modernized London, Haussmann widened streets, created public parks and transportation systems, and developed sophisticated sewage systems that dispatched water into new buildings. To give Paris its distinctive persona, he took inspiration from architect Andrea Palladio (1508–80), who stunned Europe with his insistence on proportional relationships and documented his beliefs in *The Four Books of Architecture*.

Haussmann's construction laws specified building heights and street widths. While limiting exteriors to six floors, he demanded that each interior be a *minimum* of 2.6 meters high—or for American purposes, nearly nine feet tall. Each new block was kept to a visual standard with windows of equal size, balconies on the second and fifth floors dressed in beautiful iron railings, and fluid moldings giving a disciplined look to the street. Only on close examination was it clear that details in stonework and doors differed from building to building. His restrictions effectively shaped interiors with the latest conveniences—running water, gas lighting, elevators—plus generous entrance halls, beautiful floors, marble mantels, and coveted natural light streaming through every window.

Seeing green? That's because it is serene, the hue we crave during difficult times, say color experts. Sofa from Cache is upholstered in fabric from Nancy Corzine, both in Los Angeles. The Aubusson area rug is from the Arcadia Rug Company, Houston.

The buildings we associate most strongly with Paris are Haussmann creations, scaled–down versions of the aristocratic *hôtel particulier,* designed for the middle class—a segment of the Parisian population that grew rapidly during the nineteenth century.

Left: Koplavitch & Zimmer smatters mini-pearls – once believed to promote marital bliss – on pillows and the bedskirt. Brunschwig & Fils distributes the romantic silk brocade from Veral de Belval, Paris. Bed is custom.

Designed for a true diva, is a dressing room inspired by Paris's Chanel Boutique, bedecked in absolute black and tea rose marble floors and black lacquer cabinetry. A settee in bad repair found at the Paris Flea Market now boasts an Old World Weavers cut velvet edged in an Ellen Holt trim. In 1926, Gabrielle "Coco" Chanel (1883–1971) introduced the little black dress today fashionable everywhere. But her influence in the design world is less well known. Clients, friends, and decorators took note of how she furnished her rooms.

Opposite: What better place to put the world on hold than in a shampoo room where one can nibble strawberries dipped in chocolate and have a glass of Dom Perignon while admiring the surroundings? The fixtures are Lalique. At the glass works in Wingen-sur-Moder, in the Alsace region of eastern France, artisans pull molten glass from ancient furnaces, toiling until the lead crystal glitters, and then finishing each exquisitely crafted piece with the company's carefully etched signature. Although best known for his superb glass works, founder Rene Lalique's career began as a jeweler.

Paris

"It is in Paris that the beating of Europe's heart is felt."
—Victor Hugo

A Lalique pattern inspired the etched glass on a staircase, offering light in a tight space.

Opposite: A carpeted curved staircase inspired by Coco Chanel's circular stairs on the rue Cambon - the perch from which she observed her fashions parade - leads to the closet's second floor rather than the designer's famous apartment above the Chanel shop. The gathering of framed black-and-white drawings was a gift to the homeowner from the late Frank Olive, the hat designer.

With its historic monuments, ancient fountains and towering stone façades, we are irresistibly drawn to the elegance of Paris, the hub of political, economic, educational, cultural, and fashionable French life. Besotted with everything from the ancient capital's sinful cuisine, to its museums, to its mannerly dogs, it is little wonder that many of us fail to notice the bronze plaque centered in an open square in front of the glorious Cathédrale Notre-Dame—begun in 1163 and completed approximately one hundred years later. But, then, the landmark is hard to spot unless one knows it is there. Set in the remnants of medieval streets, it marks *"Point Zero Des Routes De France"*—shedding light on how the French have long viewed their capital.

Although the Cathédrale is not the geographical center of the *Hexagone,* as the people often refer to their country, from here all distances in France have been measured for several centuries. With the capital being the center of much of the country's wealth and power, it is from this point that roads and rivers crisscrossing the country assertively calculate the distance (in kilometers) between Paris and other cities. It is an unbending rule that trains with even numbers *(pair)* travel to Paris, those with odd numbers *(impair)* away. The French do not say that they are going to or from Paris, but rather that they are going up to Paris or down from Paris, underscoring the love they feel for their capital as well as its importance—and the chasm that exists between Paris and the countryside.

An important early-nineteenth-century French clock stands atop a black lacquer mantel with gold leaf, the latter a copy of one that adorned the *Titanic*, which sank on her maiden voyage ninety some years ago. In the seventeenth century, clocks were a new invention. Louis XIV provided lodging at the Louvre for his favorite clockmakers and gave them unique status at court. Today the area surrounding Besançon, France, is world renowned for its excellent clockmakers.

Left: Nancy Corzine cut velvet wraps the walls of a striking men's powder room. Fittings are Sherle Wagner, New York. The antique swan sconces came from Paris. For all the apparent affluence at the royal palace, only Louis XIV had the use of a proper bathroom with running water.

In the kitchen stands a wine bar touting cheese. There are upwards of five hundred varieties of cheese in France, with Brie and Camembert among the most popular. For these, the country relies on *affineurs*, or ripeners, who age and finish various *fromages* in temperature- and humidity- controlled caves, taking care to turn each cheese as required, or wash the rinds as they cure. Alleose, Barthelemy, and Marie-Anne Cantin are three of the best cheese shops in Paris.

Opposite: Once most servants' kitchens were on the ground floor of *chateaux* – far from dining rooms to avoid scattering fires, sounds, and aromas – places most would seldom go. Though inspiration for this room's design came from these very kitchens, the space here is more readily imagined filled with guests complementing the chef. The *piece de resistance* is a porcelain-enameled La Cornue range, the *creme de la creme* of stoves – acclaimed by French gourmets since 1908.

Inspired by the Plate Hall at Château de Fontainebleau, outside Paris is a Hall of Plates here in the states.

Left: An artfully composed grouping of Louis XV and XVI gilt wood mirrors discovered on the quai Voltaire adds romance and luster. The satinwood *enfilade* with tulipwood marquetry is nineteenth century, wearing original bronze fittings and original marble top.

An eagle soars through the seventy-eight-foot-high dome of a home inspired by Vaux-le-Vicomte, the grand seventeenth-century *château* of Nicholas Fouquet, Minister of Finance under Louis XIV. A rooftop terrace offers an excellent view of the estate.

Opposite: Seeing is not necessarily believing when it comes to *trompe l'oeil*. With roots in Greek and Roman times, it tampers with perceptions, or "tricks the eye." This romantic landscape also delights the heart, reshaping a stairwell by making flat surfaces appear three-dimensional.

Above: In 1785, King Louis XVI sent an expedition to Australia, where the group collected exotic plants and animals. Among the birds brought to back to France were parakeets, crested cockatoos, and black swans. Later, Josephine would adopt the swan as her symbol, incorporating it into the decor of Malmaison, her country home. Napoleon's personal symbol was the bee, though swans also decorated objects made for him.

Left: If there were an award for the most opulent theater, one patterned after the Paris Opera House would surely receive the honor, thanks to its carpet from the French company Braquenie – founded in 1823 and now owned by Pierre Frey – gold-leaf moldings, and silk curtains from Old World Weavers. Unseen are curtains flanking the stage, a velvet from Travers, Inc. Each spring, the Cannes Film Festival awards its Palme d'Or (Golden Palm) for the best film.

In the eighteenth century, nothing was considered quite as offensive as a natural look. Ladies favored an icy pallor, rouged cheeks and lips, and towering coiffures, which at times reached such heights that they were forced to travel with their heads outside carriage windows. Fabric in women's powder room is Charles Burger Paris for Quadrille. Sinks and rose quartz fittings are from Sherle Wagner.

A conservatory's French sink – filled with tulips and daffodils – once served as a fountain.

Opposite: The sheet press, now in vogue, gives fresh respectability to a laundry room.

A *World* AWAY

Without a royal family in our midst since America won her freedom, we pledged undying loyalty to one French king—assisting him in creating an empire that stretched from Paris to New York. Considered *le dernier cri,* or the last word, in style, then, was living contentedly amid furnishings honoring a sole celebrated monarch known for his tony addresses.

But not long ago we began looking beyond the familiar, in keeping with the ethos of the times. Travel to foreign lands, interest in world affairs, and passion for the decorative arts opened our minds to new centers of influence—offering ample evidence that furnishings from different eras and unlikely places were well worth harboring, plus much more chic. Now, an unshakable commitment to one long-dead ruler is no longer the inhibiting force it once was, challenging our intentions.

Despite lingering political differences, our ardor for Fine French Furnishings remains. A survey by the trade magazine *Home Décor Buyer* found that sixty-six percent of Americans prefer their furnishings French—more than any other style. If Washington, D.C. can accept the high-mindedness that makes the French, well, French, we can scarcely be considered unpatriotic for installing Gallic beauty.

Besides, no one says, these days, that a mansion with multiple fireplaces must pay unbending reverence to a sole sovereign, or that a house more upscale than its modest looks imply cannot be open to disparate, widespread influences, reflecting the world that we inhabit.

Plainly, somewhere between the twentieth and twenty-first centuries, the purist look lost its panache, replaced by newly defined foreign policies rising from the old.

A *World* AWAY

Preceding Overleaf: In a living room overlooking the Golden Gate Bridge, chairs from sundry families mingle at a marriage of the young and the old, the high and the low – all from Ambiance Antiques. San Francisco. The walnut *buffet a deux corps* and Regence end table date from the eighteenth century. The period child's chair wears a Christopher Norman check.

Opposite: A new construction inspired by the eighteenth-century style *de la reine* exudes noble airs, painting the house with further importance.

A monochromatic storytelling toile hugs stateside walls while a nineteenth-century Louis XVI dressing table helps turn a guest room into a *boudoir*, which is French for 'place to pout or sulk.' The pair of Canton lamps flanking the painted mirror once belonged to Franklin Delano Roosevelt and his wife Eleanor.

Opposite: Surely, this imperial blue-and-white guest room would have been the envy of Marie Antoinette, who was passionate for toile. The French, like people in other Mediterranean countries, also lay great store in the color blue, believing it can keep all manner of misfortune away, as well as spurn flies in regions where screens rarely grace windows or doors.

Putting our diplomatic skills to the test, we exercise freedom of choice, unapologetically channeling our artistry, energy, and resources in fresh design directions while giving equal weight to comfort and glamour appropriately tailored to our principles as well as the demands of American life. At the end of the day, the past lives side by side with heirlooms-in-the-making, in settings reflecting our comings and goings—better known as buying trips.

Fashioning ties with a mélange of cultures igniting curiosity, we layer hand-loomed Portuguese needlepoint rugs, Italian bed frames, plus discarded German trunks brimming with hard-to-resist Hungarian china, beguiling Swiss lace, and English sterling silver, should more be needed. All mingle amicably with serendipitous imports already in place: glassware produced on the Venetian Island of Murano; ribbon-tied, paper-covered boxes made in Venice; folding screens from Asia, though not necessarily acquired by taking an exotic journey to the Far East. And, yes, lest we forget, American billiard tables.

Never mind that pointedly mixing cultures is a notion almost unheard-of in France, where domestic *objets d'art* are the norm with a hand-painted *secrétaire* that happens to catch one's eye being occasionally air-freighted from Italy. Savvy as we are about the ways of the world, it is only fitting, after all, that we sculpt our own artful visions of gracious living while priding ourselves on our creative differences and celebrating the liberties we enjoy.

Adorning the master bath is a Charles II embroidered writing box, circa 1660, a fine example of stumpwork trapunto, which was in vogue during the late Tudor and Jacobean periods. But a rare Chinese export pot dated 1775 vies for attention. It was made in India for the British market.

Traversing time zones and connecting cultures is a collection of silver miniatures that adds out-of-the-ordinary luster. An eighteenth-century knife box of Dutch descent is covered with shagreen (untanned skins of horses, mules or sharks dyed green) and has all its original fittings and key, plus silver hallmark knives, forks, and spoons. The crowns are nineteenth-century French. The George III (1760–1820) vase, circa 1764, is from England, of course.

Imbuing an entrance hall with style is an impressive eighteenth-century Baccarat crystal chandelier.

Who could resist sitting up and taking notice of an eighteenth-century Venetian chair, painted green? It is warmed with a seventeenth-century English needlework pillow trimmed in antique braid.

A Napoleonic ormolu and crystal chandelier, circa 1800.

Appropriately dressed for anywhere, a French child-size chair, circa 1825, wears its original needlework.

Double doors open to a light-filled foyer where a *confidante* wearing Old World Weavers fabric is clearly the center of attention. It holds court with an air of authority, while an eighteenth-century Tabriz rug from the Renaissance Collection in Dallas sprawls on wood floors. Tabriz is the capital of Azerbaijan, Iran's most populous province, bordering Turkey and the Soviet Union.

Opposite: Across the room, a painted XVI-period *bombe* commode offers fashionable ladies a place to lay their handbags.

For us, there is a feeling of satisfaction in presenting aesthetic views as different as the cities we live in, yet awash in style, function, and well-being, where even a parade of driven kings all named Louis and crowned with towering Roman numerals might reside quite happily. Even if that is not what Louis XIV or his successors had in mind back in the seventeenth century, it is hardly less impressive—or less than appropriately respectful.

Indeed, the old-world élan of our rooms owe much to secrets we have gleaned from the French. How else to explain—given our growing enthusiasm for juxtaposing pleasures from Italy, Spain, and Portugal, Great Britain, Germany, and Sweden—turning out settings *unmistakably* French, certainly worthy of France at her best?

The clock is a Paris flea-market find.

A walnut etagere – or hanging shelves for display – is a fixture in South of France homes.

Left: A Rose Cummings stripe serves as a backdrop for an eighteenth-century *trumeau* with *trophee* from Jean Newhart Antiques in Los Gatos, California. The chaise is nineteenth-century in the style of Louis XV. Toile-covered storage boxes are tied with grosgrain ribbon.

Directory

Here is where to find the designers mentioned in this book . . .

Cathryn Chapman

Chapman Design

7026 Old Katy Road

Suite 163 A

Houston, TX 77024

Telephone: 713.864.8622

Facsimile: 713.864.8624

David Corley, ASID

Julie Stryker

David Corley Interior Design

1824 Market Center Boulevard

Dallas, TX 75207

Telephone: 214.742.6767

Facsimile: 214.747.9178

Cheryl Driver

C. K. Driver Design Group

713 Oak Grove Avenue

Menlo Park, CA 94025

Telephone: 650.323.4200

Facsimile: 650.323.8300

Pamela Kay Flowers, ASID

P. K. Flowers Interiors, Inc.

216 North Front Street

Aledo, TX 76008

Telephone: 817.441.3000

Facsimile: 817.441.6602

Robert P. Henry, ASID

Robert P. Henry Design Collection

6335 West Northwest Hwy, Suite 712

Dallas, TX 75225

Telephone: 214.750.8711

Facsimile: 214. 691.9829

John Kidd, Allied Member ASID

John Kidd Associates

5120 Woodway Road, Suite 7033

Houston, TX 77056

Telephone: 713.961.1888

Facsimile: 713.961.1912

Dana Moore

Dana Moore Interior Design

3901 Turtle Creek Boulevard, Suite 14

Dallas, TX 75219

Telephone: 214.528.2212

Facsimile: 214.821.4310

Molly Ogden

Molly Moon Ogden Interior Design

2217 Ward Parkway

Fort Worth, TX 76110

Telephone: 817.924.5460

Facsimile: 817.300.9222

Roberta Peters

Roberta Peters Design

172 Centre Street

Mountain View, CA 94041

Telephone: 650.960.0512

Facsimile: 650.960.0513

Betty Lou Phillips, ASID

Interiors by BLP

4278 Bordeaux Avenue

Dallas, TX 75205

Telephone: 214.599.0191

Facsimile: 214.599.0192

Christina Phillips, ASID

CMP Designs, Inc.

3513 Arborlawn Drive

Fort Worth, TX 76109

Telephone: 817.927.5210

Facsimile: 817.927.9210

Marilyn Phillips

Loren Interiors

1125 Riverbend Road

Houston, TX 77063

Telephone: 713.973.6475

Facsimile: 713.973.8859

Tony Stavish

A. W. Stavish Designs

2223 West Shakespeare Avenue, Suite 1R

Chicago, IL 60647

Telephone: 773.227.0117

Facsimile: 773.227.9057

Shelley Stevens

Orion Antique Importers, Inc.

1435 Slocum Street

Dallas, TX 75207

Telephone: 214.748.1177

Facsimile: 214.748.1491

Mersina Stubbs
Pryor Lancaster
Mersina Stubbs Interiors
3401 Main Street, Building B
Dallas, TX 75226
Telephone: 214.363.9496
Facsimile: 214.363.9497

Robert Wakefield
R. N. Wakefield & Company
2702 Westheimer Road
Houston, TX 77098
Telephone: 713.528.4677
Facsimile: 713.528.3678

Deborah Walker, ASID
Elizabeth Lank, ASID
Deborah Walker & Associates
1925 Cedar Springs Road, Suite 103
Dallas, TX 75201
Telephone: 214.521.9637
Facsimile: 214.521.9638

Rebecca Turner Wiggins
Rebecca Turner Wiggins and Associates
651 Business Loop IH/35 North,
Suite 1135
New Braunfels, TX 78130
Telephone: 830.620.7475
Facsimile: 830.629.2239

and the architects:

J. Terry Bates, AIA
J. Terry Bates & Associates, Inc.
1705 19th Avenue S.
Nashville, TN 37212
Telephone: 615.298.2288
Facsimile: 615.298.2314

What better place to discuss world affairs or the price of oil than in this soaring library, where mahogany paneling heightens the masculine air? Not so long ago, this space looked more like a master bedroom and an exercise room. That is because it was! But inspired by a magazine photograph, the homeowner sought something more. Window-covering fabric is from Grey Watkins, Ltd. Niermann-Weeks made the Neapolitan sconces.

Robbie Fusch, Architect
Fusch, Serold & Partners
5950 Berkshire Lane, Suite 1500
Dallas, TX 75225
Telephone: 214.696.0152
Facsimile: 214.696.6938

Cole Smith, FAIA
Smith, Ekblad & Associates, Inc.
2719 Laclede Street
Dallas, TX 75204
Telephone: 214.871.0305
Facsimile: 214.871.0644

Traffic from outdoors is routed through a mudroom where vintage canisters keep clutter to a minimum by holding this and that, including Band-Aids to soothe a child's wounds. Wallcovering is from Brunschwig and Fils.

Right: A farm table, woven-rush-seat chair, and a working fireplace are fixtures in the French countryside, where blue and yellow are prevailing hues.

Resources

Whether a Palm Pilot organizer, Filofax or simply an address book, it is among a designer's most important possessions; aside from combing showrooms in decorative centers, professionals are regular visitors to well-known department stores, such as Neiman Marcus, Bergdorf Goodman, Barneys New York, Bloomingdale's, and Saks Fifth Avenue. Also among our favorite stomping grounds are the retail establishments of Pierre Deux, Ralph Lauren, Crate & Barrel, Pottery Barn, Pier 1 Imports, Williams-Sonoma, and Banana Republic. Then, too, we are big believers in catalog shopping with Ballard Designs—definitely worth a second look.

Below, we share more savvy places to shop for antiques, rugs, lighting, and architectural elements similar to those shown.

ANTIQUE FURNISHINGS AND ACCESSORIES

Ambiance Antiques
135 Rhode Island Street
San Francisco, CA 94103
Telephone: 415.255.9006
www.ambianceantiques.com

America Antiques and Design
5 South Main Street
Lambertville, NJ 08530
Telephone: 609.397.6966
www.americadesigns.com

Agostino Antiques Ltd.
808 Broadway at 11th Street
New York, NY 10003
Telephone: 212.533.3355
www.agostinoantiques.com

Bremermann Designs
3943 Magazine Street
New Orleans, LA 70115
Telephone: 504.891.7763

Brian Stringer Antiques
2031 West Alabama Street
Houston, TX 77006
Telephone: 713.526.7380

Burden & Izett, Ltd.
180 Duane Street
New York, NY 10013
Telephone: 212.941.8247
www.burdenandizett.net

Carl Moore Antiques
1610 Bissonnet Street
Houston, TX 77005
Telephone: 713.524.2502
www.carlmooreantiques.com

Challiss House
463 Jackson Street
San Francisco, CA 94111
Telephone: 415.397.6999
www.challisshouse.com

Charles Gaylord Antiques
2151 Powell Street
San Francisco, CA 94133
Telephone: 415.392.6085

Château Domingue
3615-B West Alabama Street
Houston, TX 77027
Telephone: 713.961.3444
www.ChateauDomingue.com

Connoisseur Antiques
8468 Melrose Place
Los Angeles, CA 90069
Telephone: 323.658.8432
www.connoisseurantiques.com

Country French Interiors
1428 Slocum Street
Dallas, TX 75207
Telephone: 214.747.4700
www.countryfrenchinteriors.com

Dixon & Harris of Royal
237 Royal Street
New Orleans, LA 70130
Telephone: 800.848.5148
www.dixonandharris.com

Duane Antiques
176 Duane Street
New York, NY 10013
Telephone: 212.625.8066
www.duaneantiques.com

If summering along the Seine is not in one's travel plans, then make Château Domingue in Houston the next stop when looking for a treasure trove of architectural fixtures with the glow of another era. All are from villas, *chateaux,* and manor houses dotting the European countryside.

A Belvadere stoneware platter from England basks in the glow of a bronze candlestick lamp wearing a smocked lampshade with rich detailing.

Gore Dean Antiques
2828 Pennsylvania Avenue
Washington, DC 20007
Telephone: 202.625.1776
www.goredeanantiques.com

The Gray Door
1809 West Gray Street
Houston, TX 77019
Telephone: 713.521.9085

Habité Antiques
963 Harrison Street
San Francisco, CA 94107
Telephone: 415.543.3515
www.habite.com

Hideaway House
143 North Robertson Boulevard
Los Angeles, CA 90048
Telephone: 310.276.4319
www.hideawayhouse.com

Inessa Stewart Antiques
5330 Bluebonnet Boulevard
Baton Rouge, LA 70809
Telephone: 225.368.8600
www.inessa.com

Inessa Stewart Antiques
5201 West Lovers Lane
Dallas, TX 75209
Telephone: 214.366.2660
www.inessa.com

Ed Hardy San Francisco, Inc.
188 Henry Adams Street
San Francisco, CA 94103
Telephone: 415.626.6300
www.edhardysf.com

Eron Johnson Antiques, Ltd.
451 North Broadway Street
Denver, CO 80203
Telephone: 303.777.8700
www.eronjohnsonantiques.com

Fireside Antiques
14007 Perkins Road
Baton Rouge, LA 70810
Telephone: 225.752.9565
www.firesideantiques.com

The French Attic
116 Bennett Street
Atlanta, GA 30309
Telephone: 404.352. 4430
www.thestalls.com

The Gables
711 Miami Circle
Atlanta, GA 30324
Telephone: 800.753.3342
www.thegablesantiques.com

Galerie de France
184–186 Duane Street
New York, NY 10013
Telephone: 212.965.0969

Jacqueline Adams
2300 Peachtree Road NW,
Suite B 110
Atlanta, GA 30309
Telephone: 404.355.8123

Jane J. Marsden Antiques
2300 Peachtree Road, NW
Atlanta, GA 30309
Telephone: 404.355.1288
www.marsdenantiques.com

Jane Moore Interiors
2922 Virginia Street
Houston, TX 77098
Telephone: 713.526.6113

John Rosselli & Associates, Ltd.
523 East 73rd Street
New York, NY 10021
Telephone: 212.772.2137

John Rosselli & Associates, Ltd.
255 East 72nd Street
New York, NY 10021
Telephone: 212.737.2252

Joseph Minton Antiques
1410 Slocum Street
Dallas, TX 75207
Telephone: 214.744.3111
www.mintonantiques.com

Joyce Horn Antiques
1008 Wirt Road
Houston, TX 77055
Telephone: 713.688.0507

Junque
2303 A Dunlavy Street
Houston, TX 77006
Telephone: 713.529.2177

Le Louvre French Antiques
1313 Slocum Street
Dallas, TX 75207
Telephone: 214.742.2605

Legacy Antiques
1406 Slocum Street
Dallas, TX 75207
Telephone: 214.748.4606

The Lotus Collection
445 Jackson Street
San Francisco, CA 94111
Telephone: 415.398.8115
www.ktaylor-lotus.com

Made In France
2912 Ferndale Place
Houston, TX 77098
Telephone: 713.529.7949

Maison Felice
73-960 El Paseo
Palm Desert, CA 92260
Telephone: 760.862.0021
www.maisonfelice.com

Mariette Himes Gomez
506 East 74th Street
New York, NY 10021
Telephone: 212.288.6856

Marston Luce
1651 Wisconsin Avenue, NW
Washington, DC 20007
Telephone: 202.333.6800

The Mews
1708 Market Center Boulevard
Dallas, TX 75207
Telephone: 214.748.9070
www.themews.net

Newel Art Galleries, Inc.
425 East 53rd Street
New York, NY 10022
Telephone: 212.758.1970
www.newel.com

Niall Smith
306 East 61st Street
New York, NY 10021
Telephone: 212.750.3985

Nick Brock, Antiques
2909 North Henderson Street
Dallas, TX 75206
Telephone: 214.828.0624

Orion Antique Importers, Inc.
1435 Slocum Street
Dallas, TX 75207
Telephone: 214.748.1177
www.oriondallas.com

Parc Monceau, Ltd.
45 D Bennett Street, NW
Atlanta, GA 30309
Telephone: 404.355.3766

Patina Atelier Antiques
3364 Sacramento Street
San Francisco, CA 94118
Telephone: 415.409.2299

Pittet & Co.
1215 Slocum Street
Dallas, TX 75207
Telephone: 214.748.8999
www.pittet.com

Sidney Lerer
420 Richmond Avenue
Point Pleasant Beach, NJ 08741
Telephone: 732.899.8949

South of Market
345 Peachtree Hills Avenue
Atlanta, GA 30305
Telephone: 404.995.9399

Vieux Carré
546 Hudson Street
New York, NY 10014
Telephone: 212.647.7633

The Whimsey Shoppe Slocum
1444 Oak Lawn
Dallas, TX 75207
Telephone: 214.745.1800

Therien & Co.
716 North La Cienega Boulevard
Los Angeles, CA 90069
Telephone: 310.657.4615
www.therien.com

Therien & Co.
411 Vermont Street
San Francisco, CA 94103
Telephone: 415.956.8850
www.therien.com

Uncommon Market, Inc.
2701 Fairmount
Dallas, TX 75201
Telephone: 214.871.2775

Watkins, Culver, Gardner
2308 Bissonnet Street
Houston, TX 77005
Telephone: 713.529.0597

Webster House Antiques
1644 Wyandotte Street
Kansas City, MO 64108
Telephone: 816.221.4713
www.websterhousekc.com

BATH FITTINGS

Czech & Speake
350 11th Street
Hoboken, NJ 07030
Telephone: 800.632.4165
www.homeportfolio.com

Herbeau Creations of America
2725 Davis Boulevard
Naples, FL 34104
Telephone: 800.547.1608
www.herbeau.com

Kallista, Inc.
2446 Verna Court
San Leandro, CA 94577
Telephone: 888.4.Kallista
www.kallistainc.com

St. Thomas Creations, Inc.
1022 West 24th Street, Suite 125
National City, CA 91950
Telephone: 619.474.9490
www.stthomascreations.com

Sherle Wagner, International
60 East 57th Street
New York, NY 10022
Telephone: 212.758.3300
www.sherlewagner.com

Waterworks
60 Backus Avenue
Danbury, CT 06810
Telephone: 800.899.6757
www.waterworks.com

CARPETS

Asmara, Inc.
88 Black Falcon Avenue
Boston, MA 02210
Telephone: 800.451.7240
www.asmarainc.com

Beauvais Carpets
201 East 57th Street
New York, NY 10022
Telephone: 212.688.2265
www.beauvaiscarpets.com

Design Materials
241 South 55th Street
Kansas City, KS 66106
Telephone: 913.342.9796

Hokanson
Decorative Center
5120 Woodway Road
Houston, TX 77056
Telephone: 800.243.7771
www.hokansoncarpet.com

Mansour
8600 Melrose Avenue
Los Angeles, CA 90069
Telephone: 310.652.9999

Mark, Inc.
323 Railroad Avenue
Greenwich, CT 06830
Telephone: 203.861.0110
www.brunschwig.com

Nouri & Sons Antique Oriental Rugs
3845 Dunlavy Street
Houston, TX 77006
Telephone: 713.523.6626
www.nouriantiquerugs.com

Renaissance Collection
1532 Hi Line Drive
Dallas, TX 75207
Telephone: 214.698.1000
www.rencollection.com

Rosecore Carpet Co., Inc.
D&D Building
979 Third Avenue
New York, NY 10022
Telephone: 212.421.7272
www.fschumacher.com

Stark Carpet
D&D Building
979 Third Avenue
New York, NY 10022
Telephone: 212.752.9000
www.starkcarpet.com

Stephen Miller Gallery
800 Santa Cruz Avenue
Menlo Park, CA 94025
Telephone: 650.327.5040
www.stephenmillergallery.com

DECORATIVE HARDWARE

E. R. Butler & Co., Inc.
75 Spring Street, 5th Floor
New York, NY 10012
Telephone: 212.925.3565
www.erbutler.com

Nanz Custom Hardware
20 Vandam Street
New York, NY 10013
Telephone: 212.367.7000
www.nanz.com

P. E. Guerin, Inc.
21–23 Jane Street
New York, NY 10014
Telephone: 212.243.5270
www.peguerin.com

Palmer Designs
7875 Convoy Court
San Diego, CA 92111
Telephone: 858.576.1350
www.palmer-design.com

Brad Oldham
Phoenix 1 Restoration & Construction Ltd.
9411 Hargrove Street
Dallas, TX 75220
Telephone: 214.902.0111
www.phoenix1.org

FABRICS AND WALLCOVERINGS

Anna French
Classic Revivals
One Design Center Place, Suite 534
Boston, MA 02210
Telephone: 617.574.9030

Bennison Fabrics
76 Greene Street
New York, NY 10012
Telephone: 212.941.1212

Bergamo Fabrics
7 West 22nd Street, 2nd Floor
New York, NY 10011
Telephone: 212.462.1010
www.bergamofabrics.com

Brunschwig & Fils, Inc.
75 Virginia Road
North White Plains, NY 10603
Telephone: 914.684.5800
www.brunschwig.com

Carlton V
D&D Building
979 Third Avenue, 15th Floor
New York, NY 10022
Telephone: 212.355.4525

Christopher Norman, Inc.
41 West 25th Street, 10th Floor
New York, NY 10010
Telephone: 212.647.0303
www.christophernorman.com

Clarence House
211 East 58th Street
New York, NY 10022
Telephone: 212.752.2890
www.clarencehouse.com

Coraggio Textiles
1750 132nd Avenue, NE
Bellevue, WA 98005
Telephone: 425.462.0035
www.coraggio.com

Cowtan & Tout
111 Eighth Avenue, Suite 930
New York, NY 10011
Telephone: 212.647.6900

Elizabeth Dow, Ltd.
155 Sixth Avenue, 4th Floor
New York, NY 10013
Telephone: 212.219.8822
www.elizabethdow.com

Fortuny, Inc.
D&D Building
979 Third Avenue, 16th Floor
New York, NY 10022
Telephone: 212.753.7153
www.fortunyonline.com

Haas
50 Dey Street, Building One
Jersey City, NJ 07306
Telephone: 201.792.5959

Hinson & Company
2735 Jackson Avenue
Long Island City, NY 11101
Telephone: 718.482.1100

J. Robert Scott
500 North Oak Street
Inglewood, CA 90302
Telephone: 310.680.4300
www.jrobertscott.com

Jane Shelton
205 Catchings Avenue
Indianola, MS 38751
Telephone: 800.530.7259
www.janeshelton.com

Jim Thompson
1694 Chantilly Drive
Atlanta, GA 30324
Telephone: 800.262.0336
www.jimthompson.com

Lee Jofa
225 Central Avenue S.
Bethpage, NY 11714
Telephone: 888.LeeJofa
www.leejofa.com

Manuel Canovas
111 Eighth Avenue, Suite 930
New York, NY 10011
Telephone: 212.647.6900

Marvic Textiles
30–10 41st Avenue, 2nd Floor
Long Island City, NY 11101
Telephone: 718.472.9715

Nancy Corzine
256 West Ivy Avenue
Inglewood, CA 90302
Telephone: 310.672.6775

Nobilis
57-A Industrial Road
Berkeley Heights, NJ 07922
Telephone: 800.464.6670
www.nobilis.fr

Old World Weavers
D&D Building
979 Third Avenue
New York, NY 10022
Telephone: 212.355.7186

Osborne & Little
90 Commerce Road
Stamford, CT 06902
Telephone: 203.359.1500
www.osborneandlittle.com

Payne Fabrics
1000 Fountain Parkway
Grand Prairie, TX 75050
Telephone: 800.527.2517
www.westgatefabrics.com

Peter Fasano, Ltd.
964 South Main Street
Great Barrington, MA 01230
Telephone: 413.528.6872

Pierre Frey, Inc.
12 East 33rd Street
New York, NY 10016
Telephone: 212.213.3099

Nestled in a corner off an elegant entry is a powder room that puts on the ritz. From the Sherle Wagner china sink and Louis XV antique mirror to walls luxuriantly hung in Paul Montgomery's heavy Florentine paper, there is meticulous attention to detail.

Left: Toile tablecloths adorn luncheon tables celebrating the completion of the author's latest book.

Pollack & Associates
150 Varick Street
New York, NY 10013
Telephone: 212.627.7766

Prima Seta Silks / Jagtar & Co.
3073 North California Street
Burbank, CA 91505
Telephone: 818.729.9333

Quadrille
50 Dey Street, Building One
Jersey City, NJ 07306
Telephone: 201.792.5959

Robert Allen
55 Cabot Boulevard
Mansfield, MA 02048
Telephone: 800.240.8189

Rogers & Goffigon
41 Chestnut Street
Greenwich, CT 06830
Telephone: 203.532.8068

Rose Cumming
Fine Arts Building
232 East 59th Street, 5th Floor
New York, NY 10022
Telephone: 212.758.0844

Scalamandré
300 Trade Zone Drive
Ronkonkoma, NY 11779
Telephone: 631.467.8800
www.scalamandre.com

Schumacher Company
79 Madison Avenue, 14th Floor
New York, NY 10016
Telephone: 212.213.7900
www.fschumacher.com

Silk Trading Co.
360 South La Brea Avenue
Los Angeles, CA 90036
Telephone: 323.954.9280
www.silktrading.com

Travers
504 East 74th Street
New York, NY 10021
Telephone: 212.772.2778
www.traversinc.com

FURNITURE

Cameron Collection
150 Dallas Design Center
1025 North Stemmons Freeway
Dallas, TX 75207
Telephone: 214.744.1544

Charles P. Rogers
55 West 17th Street
New York, NY 10011
Telephone: 212.675.4400
www.charlesprogers.com

Dennis & Leen
8734 Melrose Avenue
Los Angeles, CA 90069
Telephone: 310.652.0855

The Farmhouse Collection, Inc.
807 Russet Street
Twin Falls, ID 83301
Telephone: 208.736.8700

Gregorius / Pineo
653 North La Cienega Boulevard
Los Angeles, CA 90069
Telephone: 310.659.0588

Hamilton, Inc.
8417 Melrose Place
Los Angeles, CA 90069
Telephone: 323.655.9193

Jane Keltner
94 Cumberland Boulevard
Memphis, TN 38112
Telephone: 800.487.8033
www.janekeltner.com

Niermann Weeks
Fine Arts Building
232 East 59th Street
New York, NY 10022
Telephone: 212.319.7979
www.niermannweeks.com

Old Timber Table Company
908 Dragon Street
Dallas, TX 75207
Telephone: 214.761.1882

Patina, Inc.
351 Peachtree Hills Avenue, NE
Atlanta, GA 30304
Telephone: 800.635.4365
www.patinainc.com

Plenty's Horn
15 County Road 2210
Pittsburg, TX 75686
Telephone: 903.856.3609

Randolph & Hein, Inc.
2222 Palou Street
San Francisco, CA 94124
Telephone: 415.864.3371

Reynière Workshop
142 Oak Road
Monroe, NY 10950
Telephone: 845.774.1541

Rose Tarlow / Melrose House
8454 Melrose Place
Los Angeles, CA 90069
Telephone: 323.653.2122
www.rosetarlow.com

Shannon & Jeal
722 Steiner Street
San Francisco, CA 94117
Telephone: 415.563.2727
www.s-j.com

Smith & Watson
200 Lexington Avenue, Suite 801
New York, NY 10016
Telephone: 212.686.6444
www.smith-watson.com

Summer Hill, Ltd.
2682 Middlefield Road
Redwood City, CA 94063
Telephone: 650.363.2600
www.summerhill.com

Michael Taylor Designs
1500 Seventeenth Street
San Francisco, CA 94107
Telephone: 415.558.9940
www.michaeltaylordesigns.com

GARDEN ORNAMENTS

Archiped Classics
315 Cole Street
Dallas, TX 75207
Telephone: 214.748.7437
www.archipedclassics.com

New apothecary jars from Vagabond in Atlanta garnish a kitchen.

Barbara Israel Garden Antiques
296 Mount Holly Road
Katonah, NY 10536
Telephone: 212.744.6281
Facsimile: 212.744.2188
www.bi-gardenantiques.com
By appointment only.

Elizabeth Street Garden & Gallery
1176 Second Avenue
New York, NY 10021
Telephone: 212.644.6969
www.elizabethstreetgallery.com

Lexington Gardens
1011 Lexington Avenue
New York, NY 10021
Telephone: 212.861.4390

Tancredi & Morgan
7174 Carmel Valley Road
Carmel Valley, CA 93923
Telephone: 831.625.4477

Treillage, Ltd.
418 East 75th Street
New York, NY 10021
Telephone: 212.535.2288

INTERIOR ORNAMENTATION

J. P. Weaver
941 Air Way
Glendale, CA 91201
Telephone: 818.500.1740

IRON WORK

Brun Metal Crafts, Inc.
2791 Industrial Lane
Bloomfield, CO 80020
Telephone: 303.466.2513

Ironies
2222 Fifth Street
Berkeley, CA 94710
Telephone: 510.644.2100

Murray's Iron Work
5915 Blackwelder Street
Culver City, CA 90232
Telephone: 866.649.4766

Potter Art Metal
4500 North Central Expressway
Dallas, TX 75206
Telephone: 214.821.1419
www.potterartmetal.com

LIGHTING, LAMPS, AND CUSTOM LAMPSHADES

Ann Morris Antiques
239 East 60th Street
New York, NY 10022
Telephone: 212.755.3308

Bella Shades / Bella Copia
255 Kansas Street
San Francisco, CA 94103
Telephone: 415.255.0452

Chameleon
231 Lafayette Street
New York, NY 10012
Telephone: 212.343.9197

Paul Ferrante, Inc.
8464 Melrose Place
Los Angeles, CA 90069
Telephone: 323.653.4142

Marvin Alexander, Inc.
315 East 62nd Street, 2nd Floor
New York, NY 10021
Telephone: 212.838.2320

Murray's Iron Work
5915 Blackwelder Street
Culver City, CA 90232
Telephone: 310.839.7737

Nesle
151 East 57th Street
New York, NY 10022
Telephone: 212.755.0515
www.dir-dd.com/nesle.html

Niermann Weeks
Fine Arts Building
232 East 59th Street, 1st Floor
New York, NY 10022
Telephone: 212.319.7979
www.niermannweeks.com

Panache
719 North La Cienega Boulevard
Los Angeles, CA 90069
Telephone: 310.652.5050

LINENS

E. Braun & Co.
717 Madison Avenue
New York, NY 10021
Telephone: 212.838.0650

Casa Del Bianco
866 Lexington Avenue
New York, NY 10021
Telephone: 212.249.9224

Frette
799 Madison Avenue
New York, NY 10021
Telephone: 212.988.5221

Leontine Linens
804 Webster Street
New Orleans, LA 70118
Telephone: 504.899.7833

Léron Linens
750 Madison Avenue
New York, NY 10021
Telephone: 212.249.3188

Peacock Alley
1825 Market Center Boulevard
Suite 440
Dallas, TX 75207
Telephone: 214.744.0399

D. Porthault, Inc.
18 East 69th Street
New York, NY 10021
Telephone: 212.688.1660

Pratesi
4344 Federal Drive, Suite 100
Greensboro, NC 27410
Telephone: 336.299.7377

Yves Delorme
1725 Broadway
Charlottesville, VA 22902
Telephone: 800.322.3911
www.yvesdelorme.com

STONE AND TILE

Ann Sacks Tile & Stone
8120 NE 33rd Drive
Portland, OR 97211
Telephone: 800.969.5217
www.annsacks.com

Country Floors
15 East 16th Street
New York, NY 10003
Telephone: 212.627.8300
www.countryfloors.com

Paris Ceramics
151 Greenwich Avenue
Greenwich, CT 06830
Telephone: 888.845.3487
www.parisceramics.com

Renaissance Tile & Bath
349 Peachtree Hills Avenue, NE
Atlanta, GA 30305
Telephone: 800.275.1822

Walker Zanger
8901 Bradley Avenue
Sun Valley, CA 91352
Telephone: 877.611.0199
www.walkerzanger.com

Only vaguely reminiscent of the armless, backless settee from which the privileged sultan of the vast Ottoman Empire ruled during the fourteenth century is an heir to the ottoman name. These days, many applaud its versatility. Not only does it offer extra seating, but also doubles as a coffee table in some homes. The tapestry and trim are both from Clarence House Imports.

TRIMMINGS AND PASSEMENTERIE

Ellen S. Holt, Inc.
1013 Slocum Street
Dallas, TX 75207
Telephone: 214.741.1804

Houlès USA Inc.
8584 Melrose Avenue
Los Angeles, CA 90069
Telephone: 310.652.6171
www.houles.com

Kenneth Meyer Company
325 Vermont Street
San Francisco, CA 94103
Telephone: 415.861.6364

Le Potager
108 West Brookdale Place
Fullerton, CA 92832
Telephone: 714.680.8864

Leslie Hannon Custom Trimmings
665 Vetter Lane
Arroyo Grande, CA 93420
Telephone: 805.489.8400

Renaissance Ribbons
PO Box 699
Oregon House, CA 95961
Telephone: 530.692.0842
www.renaissanceribbons.com

Tassels & Trims
232 East 59th Street
New York, NY 10022
Telephone: 212.754.6000

West Coast Trimming
7100 Wilson Avenue
Los Angeles, CA 90001
Telephone: 323.587.0701

Much like in a great manor house in Europe, flowers await a cherished young guest. Twin bed is an antique.

Vin de la Suisse. elle est partagée en deux comtés, Ne
de superieur non sũt ... le t̃t̃, ... mesme dans le sptel
maison de Fribourg ... ... ar mesme moyen dans cell
un surcroist de bonk

La Description

de la Principauté
de Neufchâtel &
de Valangin

L'étendüe en
auquel elle
de la Suisse
superieur non
de Fribourg
urcroist de bonk

la France.
peuplées, le la
meilleur Vin
point de
dans la maison
avec un

le Duc de Longueville

Son aimable frère,

le Ciel me donna

Altesse, avec tous ses —
vantages, J'ai crû —
e'ont moins qu'avec —

le Duc de Long
Son aimable
m'acorder en so

La Description

L'étendüe en   de la Principauté   la France.
auquel elle   peuplées, le la
de la Suisse   de Neufchâtel &   meilleur Vin
superieur non   point de
de Fribourg   de Valangin   dans la maiso
urewist de honk   auec un

le Duc de Longueville

Son aimable frère,

le Ciel me donna

...tesse, auec tous ses — le Duc de Long
...ntages, J'ai crû — Son aimable
...nt moins qu'auec — m'acorder en so

Photographic Credits

Here are the photographic credits:

DESIGNERS:

Cathryn Chapman: 118, 119, 120, 121, 124, 130

David Corley, ASID and Julie Stryker: 150-151, 152, 154, 155, 156-157, 158, 159, 160, 161, 162-163, 164, 165, 166-167, 168, 169, 170-171, 172-173, 174, 175, 205

Cheryl Driver: 140, 142, 143, 144-145, 148-149

Pamela Kay Flowers, ASID: 184, 185

Robert P. Henry, ASID: 96, 97, 98, 99, 194

John Kidd, Allied Member ASID: 26-27, 28, 30, 31, 32, 33, 34, 35, 36, 38, 39, 40, 41, 109

Dana Moore: 180, 181, 182, 183

Molly Ogden: 72, 73, 75, 76-77, 78, 79, 80, 82-83, 84-85, 112, Back Jacket

Roberta Peters: 42, 43, 45, 46, 47, 48-49, 50, 51, 52, 54, 55, 56, 57, 100, 101, 103, 104, 106, 107, 176-177, 186-187

Betty Lou Phillips, ASID: 200-201

Christina Phillips, ASID: 14-15, 122, 123, 147

Marilyn Phillips: 58, 60-61, 62, 63, 64, 65, 66, 68, 69, 70, 71, 189

Tony Stavish: 125, 126, 127, 128, 129, 206-207

Shelley Stevens: 16, 18, 19, 20, 21, 22, 23, 24-25

Mersina Stubbs and Pryor Lancaster: 86-87, 88, 90-91, 92, 93, 94, 95, 134, 199, 203

Robert Wakefield: 114, 115, 116, 117, 194

Deborah Walker and Elizabeth Lank: Front Jacket, Opposite Table of Contents, 8, 10-11, 12, 108, 110-111, 132, 133, 135, 136, 137

Rebecca Wiggins: 190-191

ARCHITECTS:

J. Terry Bates, AIA: 150-151, 152, 154, 158, 159, 160, 161, 162-163, 164, 165, 166-167, 168, 169, 170-171

Robbie Fusch, Architect: 8, 10-11, 12, 14-15, 108, 110-111, 123, 147

Cole Smith, FAIA: 178

PHOTOGRAPHERS:

Janet Lenzen: 9, 114, 115, 116, 117, 118, 119, 120, 121, 124, 130, 189

Jeffrey Millies for Hedrich Blessing Photographers: 125, 126, 127, 128, 129, 206-207

Dan Piassick: Front Jacket, Back Jacket, Title Pages, Opposite Copyright, Opposite Table of Contents, 8, 10-11, 12, 14-15, 16, 18, 19, 20, 21, 22, 23, 24-25, 26-27, 28, 30, 31, 32, 33, 34, 35, 36, 38, 39, 40, 41, 42, 43, 45, 46, 47, 48-49, 50, 51, 52, 54, 55, 56, 57, 58, 60-61, 62, 63, 64, 65, 66, 68, 69, 70, 71, 72, 73, 75, 76-77, 78, 79, 80, 82-83, 84-85, 86-87, 88, 90–91, 92, 93, 94, 95, 96, 97, 98, 99, 100, 101, 103, 104, 106, 107, 108, 109, 100-111, 112, 122, 123, 132, 133, 134, 135, 136, 137, 141, 142, 143, 144-145, 147, 148–149, 150-151, 152, 154, 155, 156-157, 158, 159, 160, 161, 162-163, 164, 165, 166-167, 168, 169, 170- 171, 172-173, 174, 175, 176–177, 178, 180, 181, 182, 183, 184, 185, 186-187, 190-191, 194, 200-201,203, 205

COMPLIMENTARY PHOTOGRAPHY:

Château Domingue: 138, 193, 197